THE PRACTICE MANAGER LIBRARY

Managing and Communicating
your questions answered

Lyn Longridge

RADCLIFFE MEDICAL PRESS

Radcliffe Medical Press Ltd
18 Marcham Road, Abingdon, Oxon OX14 1AA, UK

British Library Cataloguing in Publication Data

A catalogue record for this book is available from the British Library

ISBN 1 85775 233 3

Library of Congress Cataloging-in-Publication Data is available.

Typeset by Acorn Bookwork, Salisbury, Wiltshire
Printed and bound by Biddles Ltd, Guildford and King's Lynn

Contents

About the author

Lyn Longridge has worked in general practice since the 1980s, starting her career in Devon. In 1993, she took up writing as a second career writing articles on management for *Practice Manager*, the *BMA News Review*, *GP*, *Croner Publications* and *Financial Pulse*. In 1996 Lyn was invited to serve on the editorial board of *Practice Manager*. She is a member of the General Practitioner Writers Association who promote the work of their writers, mostly GPs, on all subjects.

Lyn is now a freelance consultant on practice management and offers training in the use of the McLean McNicoll GP Accounts package. She runs training courses for managers under the auspices of the West Oxfordshire College and Hadzor Health Consultancy near Droitwich.

Acknowledgements

I should like to thank Dr Andrew Scott who first introduced me to the esoteric world of practice management and inveigled me into managing his practice in Devon. To the GPs and staff at that practice, and in particular the practice nurse Alison Smitheram, and to all those with whom I worked subsequently at the Church Street Surgery in Tewkesbury, I give my thanks for their support over the years.

I am grateful to Brenda Evans at *Practice Manager* who published my first article in 1993 and gave me the confidence to embark on a second career as a writer. I should also like to thank her successor as editor at *Practice Manager*, Madeleine Price, for inviting me to serve on the editorial board of that journal and for being so supportive in recent years.

To my son Edward, who is a practice manager in Dorset, and my son Christopher, who works in publishing in London, I give thanks for their existence and for their help and professional advice in the writing of this book.

Lyn Longridge
November 1997

Abbreviations

AMGP	Association of Managers in General Practice
AMSPAR	Association of Medical Secretaries, Practice Administrators and Receptionists
BMA	British Medical Association
BMJ	British Medical Journal
BNF	British National Formulary
CHC	Community Health Council
CHS	Child Health Surveillance
CPN	Community Psychiatric Nurse
DDA	Dangerous Drugs Act
DHA	District Health Authority
DoH	Department of Health
DSS	Department of Social Security
FPA	Family Planning Association
FRCGP	Fellow of the Royal College of General Practitioners
FRCOG	Fellow of the Royal College of Obstetricians and Gynaecologists
GMC	General Medical Council
GMSC	General Medical Services Committee
GMP	General Medical Practitioner
HV	Health Visitor
IHSM	Institute of Health Services Management
LMC	Local Medical Committee

MAAG	Medical Audit Advisory Group
MB	Bachelor of Medicine
MD	Doctor of Medicine
MDU	Medical Defence Union
MIMS	Monthly Index of Medical Specialities
MPS	Medical Protection Society
MRCP	Member of Royal College of Physicians of London
MRCS	Member of Royal College of Surgeons of England
NAHAT	National Association of Health Authorities and Trusts
NBTS	National Blood Transfusion Service
NHS	National Health Service
OT	Occupational Therapist
OTC	Over-the-counter
PACT	Prescribing Analysis and Costs
PGEA	Postgraduate Educational Allowance
PPG	Patient Participation Group
QALY	Quality Adjusted Life Year
RCGP	Royal College of General Practitioners
RCN	Royal College of Nursing
RHA	Regional Health Authority
SEN	State Enrolled Nurse
SHO	Senior House Officer
TQM	Total Quality Management
UKCC	United Kingdom Central Council for Nursing, Midwifery and Health Visiting
WHO	World Health Organization

To Edward and Christopher

Introduction

This book is the first in *The Practice Manager Library* intended to offer information to practice managers who are wondering how they can extend their present role, or for those new to general practice who want to know what the job might involve.

As you will no doubt have realized by now, general practice is a very unusual business – it is certainly unlike any other I have come across. Offering a service that is free on demand presents problems that are peculiar to the health service. On the one hand the business/practice has to strive to offer the best possible service to its customers/patients and on the other hand it is required to make a profit if the partners are to receive an adequate income. Few GPs are salaried, most choosing to work as self-employed independent contractors in single-handed practices or, more commonly, in partnerships where the majority of their income is derived from capitation fees and individual items of service claims. If the business is not well managed, however hard the GPs and nurses work, the patients will not receive the best possible service and the partners' income will almost certainly suffer.

In recent years general practitioners have been encouraged by government to be more businesslike. Since 1990 we have seen the introduction of the New Contract for GPs with its emphasis on health promotion and disease prevention together with a requirement to meet specific targets for immunizations and cervical cytology. The purchaser/provider split and opportunity for practices to hold their own budgets followed on from this. Currently more than 50% of patients are registered with fundholding practices. Many of those GPs who decided not to join the scheme have banded together to form locality commissioning groups in the hope that it would enable them to negotiate improved services with hospital trusts from a position of greater strength.

The Labour Government has stated its opposition to fund-holding and plans to abolish the inequities that can occur when some practices hold their own budgets and others do not. Their aim is that all practices should take part in locality commissioning which should mean that the GPs are still able to influence trusts to provide the services they need for their patients. However, it is intended that the inevitable bureaucracy and expense that fund-holding creates will be phased out.

Practice managers come from a variety of backgrounds. Some, mostly men, who were previously in the armed forces or commerce, have attempted to transfer their management skills to a second career in general practice. However, the experience they gained in such different circumstances has not always transferred well into general practice. The culture of general practice is obviously very different from that found in other organizations such as the armed forces, or indeed in a commercial organization such as a bank. Adapting to this change in organizational culture can be one of the hardest parts of the job.

Managers who have worked elsewhere in the NHS or for other non-profit-making institutions are also occasionally enticed into working in general practice. They may feel that the sideways move offers them the chance to escape from the constraints imposed by the inevitable hierarchy of hospital management and gives them the opportunity to try out a very different style of management in a small team. They have the experience of the NHS but only in the secondary care sector and it can be quite a revelation for them to be in charge of primary care services in general practice at the sharp end.

Increasingly, there are now graduates taking up a career in practice management, attracted by the idea of working virtually autonomously and with wide responsibility in a small business. It is particularly attractive to those people who want to work in the rural area where they live and do not want to commute to a large city. There are few managerial jobs to be found in villages and general practice is a welcome exception.

However, in addition to these personnel who may well have a management qualification and presumably have already acquired some management skills, there are also those practice managers who have no experience of management at all but know pretty well how general practice works. They will have risen through the ranks, having worked previously as a receptionist, medical secretary or practice nurse. The transition for them is not necessarily smooth either as they have new skills to learn and a new role to play.

Given this wide spread of experience and expertise it is obvious that individuals' need for information will be very different. However, most of those new to the job of practice manager will want to know just what the job involves, and how it differs from management in the outside world. Those who have worked in another capacity in general practice may understand the language and jargon used and know what 'GMS', 'PPA', 'GPFC' and 'CPN' stand for. (A list of common abbreviations is included for those who do not.) However, they may be unsure of just what is expected of them as a manager and how they should set about running a practice effectively.

The job of practice management will usually mean taking responsibility for managing everything within the practice (excluding the actual treatment of patients). Not only will you be expected to manage the practice but you will have to manage yourself and your own time as well. This is particularly so in general practice because you will be working in relative isolation for much of the time; GPs are notoriously hard-pressed and busy and usually find it difficult to make time to offer support to their staff. The practice manager, therefore, is dealt a double blow as she will need to offer such support to the other staff, as well as being expected to work with little assistance or supervision from the doctors.

The practice manager will normally need to assume responsibility for the areas of finance, staff, premises, office administration and information technology (IT). This is a wide remit when you consider that many commercial or industrial companies have a separate personnel manager, financial expert, IT specialist and various administrators. A practice manager should expect to wear the following 'hats' at one time or another while working in general practice, in addition to the more usual ones of finance executive or human resources manager: facilitator; communicator; liaison officer; motivator; site agent; researcher; forecaster; supporter; confidante; decision-maker; quality controller; auditor; disciplinarian; networker; umpire/referee; planner; mediator; agony aunt; and of course dogsbody.

This first book includes enquiries which I have received over the years about the Primary Health Care Team (PHCT), questions about some of the specific management skills required in general practice and topics relating to communication in the widest sense. Other books in *The Practice Manager Library* will cover matters relating to administration, general practice finance and the management of practice premises and IT.

The questions that follow, and which I have attempted to answer, are just a sample of those that have been put to me by practice managers who have often been thrown in at the deep end of general practice and told by their GPs to 'sort things out' and 'get on with it'. The truth is that generally the GPs themselves are not aware of just what managing their practices should involve and so they are unlikely to be able to give much helpful guidance to their manager. The skills needed to be a good doctor are not necessarily the same as those that a manager requires.

Acquiring the necessary knowledge and expertise will take some time and it is sometimes difficult to know where to start. I hope the answers given in this book will help you to understand some of the basic requirements that you will need in the way of management and communication skills, in order to play your part effectively as practice manager. Once you have discovered just what the job involves, you can plan a training programme to ensure that you pick up any additional skills or knowledge that you may require. There are many courses now being run specifically for practice managers and your local health authority can give you information on these. Details of others are sent regularly through the post from local colleges and other course providers.

There seems to be general agreement among practice managers that I have spoken to, that the main attraction of the job is the sheer diversity of work involved – no two days are ever the same. The challenges are both great and small, and are constant. You will have the opportunity to acquire new skills and gain a wealth of management experience and certainly never have the time to be bored. You will on occasions feel harassed and frustrated but the purpose of this book is to keep those occasions to the bare minimum.

Lyn Longridge
November 1997

In the interests of clarity, throughout the book it has been assumed that all practice managers are female and all GPs male, although this is clearly not the situation in most practices.

1

The Primary
Healthcare Team

The services available in primary care have increased dramatically over recent years. GPs' lists have had to fall as the doctors come under growing pressure from their ever more demanding patients who consult far more readily and more frequently than before. The number of practice nurses employed has risen as they have been required, in addition to their normal treatment room duties, to take on the care of patients with chronic conditions such as asthma and diabetes, as well as organizing immunizations and cytology testing to ensure targets are met.

It is not uncommon for physiotherapy, acupuncture, counselling, chiropody, osteopathy and homeopathy to be available under the same roof in general practice. The number of ancillary staff required to run these busy surgeries has also increased with most practices now employing a practice manager, and many having another manager whose sole responsibility is to control the fundholding budget or the financial side of the business.

The introduction of fundholding has meant that practices are even more involved with their attached staff. They are in effect 'buying in' the service of these community staff and thus are able to influence the level and quality of service they receive. A closer association between the different professionals such as health visitors, midwives and community nurses and the GPs themselves has been a welcome consequence of this.

New managers can find it a little daunting at first trying to identify all the various clinicians and members of staff who come and go in the practice. In this section, I have attempted to describe the roles of the ones you are most likely to meet while, at the same time, answering some of the more common questions posed about who does what and for whom.

▲ Question 1: Partners: directors or coalface workers?

It is difficult to know just what role the partners should be playing running their practice. Am I being unrealistic when I expect them to take an interest in business management as well as the treatment of their patients?

General practice is one of the few businesses where the coalface workers also constitute the board of directors. It is because the GPs are having to work every day seeing patients, that they are rarely available and are often unwilling to take on a supervisory role in the running of their practices. They find it difficult to get an overview of the way the practice is developing because they are so very much involved in the day-to-day treatment of patients and the pressure this puts on them.

However, it is important that you, as practice manager, are not left alone to run the business without any support. After all, it is the GPs' practice – not yours – and as such, they should be prepared to make reasoned decisions on its development. In the answers to other questions in this book, you will find some suggestions on how to involve the doctors more in the running of the business. The reply to Question **2** makes suggestions on individual management roles that the partners might take on. Replies to questions about team-building (*see* Question **22**) and leadership (*see* Question **23**) should also help you to find ways of involving the GPs more in the management of their practice.

The occasional case of fraud perpetrated by a practice manager which is revealed in the medical press, can make GPs take time to consider whether they are monitoring the finances of their own practice adequately. They might also have cause to wonder whether in fact they have sufficient expertise to spot possible instances of embezzlement were they to occur. This is just one good reason for you to persuade the partners that they should monitor your management closely and, if necessary, encourage them to undergo some basic training in financial management.

▲ Question 2: Partners' management role

In our practice the senior partner tries to oversee all aspects of practice management but he is a busy man, and I seldom have the opportunity to sit down with him and discuss specific problems. What can we do to ensure that I have some regular support and contact with at least one of the partners?

One possible answer might be for the other partners to agree that the 'executive partner' be allowed one half day a week of protected time in order to oversee the management of the practice. He could then be sure of having time to discuss any problems you might have encountered during the previous few days. The other partners would then either have to cover for him or agree to pay for a locum in order to release the necessary time. If the doctor is also responsible for monitoring the budget, and he also uses this time for fundholding, then at least part of the expense of a locum could be repaid to the practice from the management allowance.

Another solution for many practices to this problem, however, is to divide up the various management supervisory functions among all the partners. Thus one partner would be designated the overseer of the finances, another could be allocated the responsibility for help with staff matters, another might take overall charge of the development and use of information technology within the practice, and another might help with managing the maintenance of the premises. These particular roles can be rotated after an agreed period, or the same partner can remain in charge of one particular area if that is what suits them all.

The practice manager will gain from the potential support of all the partners in this way. When a problem arises with the staff, it should be possible to have a brief meeting with the designated partner in order to get a second opinion on the best course of action to take. It is helpful if you can persuade the finances partner to do occasional random checks on the accounts so that he can reassure himself and the other partners that everything is as it should be. Too many cases of fraud have occurred in general practices because the partners have left the manager totally unsupervised. It is not fair on them, or you, if you do not have one partner who understands the financial systems you use and is able to keep an eye on things.

▲ Question 3: A new partner

Our senior partner is due to retire in six months' time. Can you offer any advice on how we might go about recruiting a new partner?

First, the partners should decide whether they actually need to replace the retiring partner. Could they manage with fewer doctors? Is the list falling? Could the practice area usefully be reduced and the list with it? Would a cheaper option be to employ an assistant or another practice nurse? If the decision is made that a new partner is required, does he have to work full-time? Would part-time or three-quarter time be acceptable instead? How about job-sharers? All these points need to be considered before actually deciding to recruit a new partner.

Once the partners have made the decision, you will need to start the recruitment process. The first step should be to consider just what sort of doctor you wish to attract to complement your team. What special clinical interests might you wish to attract? What additional qualifications might be desirable? When you have established this, you can consider advertising. You will need to word your advertisement carefully in order to attract suitable applicants. You are not permitted to specify the gender of the doctor you are seeking and should be careful not to discriminate in any way when short-listing. The *British Medical Journal* is the usual place for such an advertisement but the weekly GP newspapers such as *GP*, *Pulse* and *Doctor* (affectionately known as 'the comics') also have columns of vacancies.

Gone are the days when any partnership vacancy in a favoured part of the country attracted over 100 applicants. Today even the most attractive practice will be lucky if they receive two or three reasonable applications and some practices have advertised several times and received no response at all.

When the closing date for applications has been reached, a decision will have to be made on who will be short-listing the candidates. This will probably not be a very onerous or potentially contentious job given the probable response. However, in addition to the original job description, the partners should by now have prepared a person specification so that a suitable candidate can be found to fit into the existing team of partners. In this person spec you will have itemized all the qualifications and qualities that you require from a new partner.

You should now be ready to select a suitable interview panel. It would not be advisable for all the partners (if there are more than three) to be present at interview, although all will naturally wish to meet and have a say in the final selection process. When making the decision it is advisable to try for consensus if at all possible. It can be very difficult if the candidate chosen only by a majority of the partners is selected and the other doctors may not feel supportive of the newly appointed partner. It is preferable to choose the partners' second choice, rather than a candidate favoured by some but fiercely objected to by others.

Once the appointment is made, the partners and manager together should devise a suitable induction programme. One of the partners will need to act as mentor for the new doctor during the probationary period. If they are not familiar with the medical software, at some time prior to their starting they will need to be taken through the various protocols. One of the partners will have to tell them just what information needs to be entered on the system during consultations, and in what format. The new doctor will also need help in accessing patient data and prescribing history and will need to feel confident in their ability to print acute prescriptions during surgery.

It can also be helpful if, in addition to a GP mentor, the new partner has a member of the reception staff allocated to them who will answer any queries in the first weeks about local arrangements regarding hospital admissions, patient transport, availability of appointments and so on.

▲ Question 4: Partners at parity

I understand from a discussion the doctors had recently in a meeting, that one of the partners has not yet reached parity. What exactly does this mean?

When a new doctor joins a practice, he may or may not be invited or expected to 'buy into' the practice. If he is, he will only be asked to buy his share of the premises and any equipment used to run the business: in law he cannot, as in most other businesses, be asked to buy a share of the 'goodwill' of the practice. The goodwill is the customer loyalty, i.e. the patient list, that has been built up over time by the previous partnership.

In recognition of this, it has been the practice of GPs taking on a new partner to offer him a reduced share of the profits for a few years, the surplus then being shared among the others. For instance, if there are five partners in the practice and they receive equal profit shares, they will be receiving 20% of the profits under normal circumstances. If one of them retires and a new partner is brought in, he may be offered 80% of his anticipated one-fifth share for the first year or two. This would mean that he receives 16/100ths, and the other four will receive 21/100ths of the profits. In this way the four original partners will receive an additional 1% of profits each until the new partner is established and moves to parity, usually within two to three years.

The whole question of working up to parity, i.e. equal shares, is under review at the moment because of the scarcity of suitable applicants. Some practices are offering parity with immediate effect on appointment in order to attract the right candidate.

▲ Question 5: Job-sharing GPs

In our practice two female partners job-share but the other four (male) partners expect them to cover for each other when one is on holiday. Is this right?

Absolutely not. Job-sharers, by their very nature, are meant to be the equivalent of one full-time doctor. Not all job-sharers split the work 50:50 but many do. Either way, if one is on holiday the other should not be expected to cover for them and each should be entitled to the same number of weeks' leave as the other full-time partners. If the full-timers work 4.5 days a week and have six weeks holiday then they are entitled to 27 days holiday a year:

4.5 x 6 = 27 days.

If they each work half-time, the job-sharing doctors are both entitled to six weeks also and for them the sum is:

$2.25 \times 6 = 13.5$ days.

Cover for the absent partner should be provided in the same way as that for other absent full-time GPs in the partnership. Occasionally I have known a job-sharer to be prepared to cover extra surgeries in return for the usual locum fee but this should be an entirely voluntary and separate arrangement. The practice will almost certainly benefit from having job-sharing partners because they each usually end up doing more than half the job. In effect, the two of them together may do 110% because of the handover period and any de-briefing sessions.

Increasingly, GPs are finding job-share an attractive option, particularly – but not exclusively – women doctors who are bringing up a young family. With the current problems in the recruitment of partners to general practice, it is worthwhile for a practice to encourage job-sharers to apply for any vacancy as they can be a decided bonus.

▲ Question 6: GP registrar

The partners have told me that they wish to apply to be a training practice. Can you tell me just what this means and what will be involved?

In order to be considered as a training practice by the regional adviser at the Department of Postgraduate Medical Education, a practice will have to satisfy certain criteria. At least one of the partners will have to achieve accreditation as a trainer and, initially, he will be approved for a period not exceeding two years. This can be extended for up to five years.

To qualify, the GP trainer will have to have a patient list of

2000 patients (or 1500 in a rural area). The practice will have to ensure that all patient notes have been suitably summarized – this involves pruning unnecessary duplication of results (many are now held on computer) and a card containing a brief summary of the patient's medical history should be placed at the front of the notes. The practice will be required to have a library of clinical textbooks available for reference and there will need to be adequate supervisory cover for the trainee doctor when he is on call.

GP registrars were previously known as GP trainees. However this was considered to be misleading since the doctors are fully qualified in medicine by the time they come to work in general practice. They join a vocational training scheme in the region for three years, one year of which will be spent in a practice and the rest in six month stints in various hospital specialties. They will be permitted a half-day release from the practice each week in order to attend sessions with their peers working in other local practices. These tutorials are known affectionately as 'playschool' by everyone.

The trainer is paid an annual fee for training the registrar and in return is expected to supervise the work of the new doctor and to make time for regular tutorials. The registrar will be expected to take his share of duty during out-of-hours and to make home visits as required. The expenses of the GP registrar such as salary, NIC and car allowance are reimbursed fully by the health authority.

In recent years there has been a significant reduction in the number of doctors opting for general practice. For this reason it is important that you make your practice as attractive as possible when trying to attract a GP registrar. You cannot change the location of your practice but you can ensure that the staff are helpful and supportive and that the partners do not 'dump' all the unwelcome tasks on to the registrar. The registrar's on-call commitment and holiday entitlement should not be less than that of the other doctors and his study leave entitlement will be greater.

For further details of the exact requirements of becoming a training practice and taking on a GP registrar, I suggest you refer to the *General Practitioners Handbook* edited by Norman Ellis.[1]

▲ Question 7: Locums

Once a locum has worked at our practice, we never seem to be able to persuade them to return again. Can you suggest where we might be going wrong?

Locums are an expensive necessity for many practices and there is usually a greater demand than can be fulfilled by those under-taking this work. It is therefore a sellers' market and it will pay you to do everything you can, not only to attract locums but to encourage them to return.

When you telephone a locum and seek their agreement to do a two-hour surgery, or to be on-call for a given night, you should always confirm the arrangement in writing. The letter should include the date, length of surgery or on-call commitment, fee agreed and availability or otherwise of on-call accommodation. Fees can vary but the BMA suggested rates are a useful starting point for negotiation.

When the locum arrives, he should be greeted and shown to the consulting room that he will be using. If he is new to the practice he will need to be given a list of internal telephone numbers and those of the local chemist, hospitals, pathology lab and so on. He will also need to be shown how to access patients' notes on the computer and be told just what information the partners wish him to enter on to the computer during consultations. It is also helpful to show him around the surgery on his first visit, in particular pointing out where he can find the nurses' treatment room, the staff WC and the GPs' staffroom where he can obtain coffee.

If you have agreed that he will do a two-hour surgery you should warn him of the number of patients he will be expected to see in that time. Some GPs have 10 minute appointments, others can see as many as 10 patients in an hour. Either way he should know that he will be required to see the agreed number in the given time to avoid any possible argument about the two-hour surgery turning out to be three hours. It is obviously unfair to expect the locum to see extras at the end of his surgery, unless additional remuneration is offered to cover the extra time.

If the locum is expected to do some home visits or to be on duty out-of-hours, he will need a map of the practice area and may ask for the use of a basic medical kit which will contain the usual equipment, drugs and injectables that a GP carries in his medical bag. Alternatively, the locum may be prepared to use his own stocks and simply ask for replacement of those he has had to use during his period working for the surgery.

It is important that you pay the locum the agreed fee promptly. In my experience locums seldom remember to provide invoices and it might be helpful if you produce two copies yourself, giving him one and asking him to receipt the other for your own records. If you treat the locum well and show that you value his contribution to the practice, he is more likely to want to return.

▲ Question 8: Retained doctor scheme

I heard of a practice locally who employs a woman GP under the retained doctor scheme which sounded an ideal way of having an extra female doctor working in the practice. Can you explain how the system works?

The Department of Health (DoH) has been anxious to assist doctors who are taking a career break to keep up-to-date with the latest developments in general practice. The doctor may be unable to consider joining a partnership at the time because of family commitments, but may wish to keep in touch with general practice. The DoH established the retained doctor scheme which permits such doctors – usually but not exclusively women – to work for up to one day a week in a practice. The practice will be reimbursed quarterly by the health authority the sum of £44.70 for one notional session per week. This session represents three and a half hours and could be split into two separate surgeries if this is what is agreed between the practice and the doctor. The practice pays the doctor an agreed amount (negotiable between the two parties) for the duties performed and the health authority pays the reduced medical defence subscription for the retained doctor.

The practice gains the help of an experienced doctor, albeit for only one or two surgeries a week, at very little cost to them. If, as in many practices, there is a preponderance of male GPs in the practice, the employment of a woman doctor under the scheme can offer patients the welcome opportunity to consult a female GP.

The retained doctor benefits because she is able to practise medicine, maintain contact with colleagues in general practice and is actively encouraged by the DoH to attend training courses to enable her to keep up-to-date with the latest developments in patient care and general practice.

▲ Question 9: Ancillary staff and attached staff

Please can you explain what the difference is between the ancillary and attached staff? I understand that not all of them are employed directly by the GPs but which are and which are not?

Ancillary staff are those employed by the practice and include practice nurses, medical secretaries, practice managers and receptionists. They will be on the practice payroll and a proportion of their salaries will normally be reimbursed to the GPs by the health authority. The government has always acknowledged that general practice is very labour-intensive and, historically, 70% of staff salaries were reimbursed in recognition of this but this level of reimbursement is no longer standard. Although reimbursement of 70% of salaries of practice staff employed prior to 1991 is protected, if they leave and are replaced there is no guarantee that the practice will receive the same level of reimbursement.

District nurses, midwives, health visitors and community psychiatric nurses (CPNs) on the other hand are not employed directly by the practice. They will generally be the employees of a local trust who will pay their salaries and also provide supervisory management. However, these community staff work with the patients of one or more of the local GP practices, are based in the community and are known as 'attached' staff. Midwives and health visitors also run regular clinics in GP surgeries for their particular client groups.

Fundholding staff, including the fund manager and computer clerks, fall into neither of the above categories, despite the fact that they are employed by the GPs. They are paid entirely out of the management allowance which is part of the fundholding scheme.

Another exception to the attached and ancillary categories is the surgery cleaner. Payment of a cleaner or cleaning agency comes out of the profits of the business which means that the doctors in effect pay for any such cleaning out of their own pockets.

▲ Question 10: Practice nurses and community nurses

In our surgery we have two part-time and one full-time practice nurse and also two district nurses attached to the practice. Can you explain to me where their duties might overlap?

Practice nurses are employed directly by the GPs and usually work only at the surgery itself and any branch surgeries the practice might have. Their salaries are usually reimbursed up to a maximum of 70% by the health authority and the employer's NIC is 100% reimbursed. Nowadays, most practices hold staff budgets which are intended to cover all ancillary staff costs (up to the 70% historical limit previously given) which has given practices the flexibility to alter the skill mix in the team. For instance, some practices have employed a phlebotomist to take blood samples from patients at a salary lower than that of many receptionists. This has released higher grade nurses (and thus more expensive staff) to undertake tasks requiring a higher level of expertise and greater responsibility.

Some practices are encouraging their more senior practice nurses to undergo additional training to qualify as nurse practitioners. This will mean that they can prescribe from a limited list of medication for patients and will take on more responsibility for the care of patients with chronic conditions.

District nurses, also known as community nurses, are employed by a local trust to look after patients in the community. Nurses are attached to a specific practice and see only those patients registered with one of the GPs. They visit housebound patients in their own homes. The community nurses liaise closely with the GPs and discuss individual cases on a regular basis. The GPs can refer any of their patients to the nurse for a visit whom they deem to be unable to attend the surgery.

A certain amount of overlap in the duties of the two teams of nurses has occurred in recent years. The requirement in the 1990 Contract for GPs to offer all patients over the age of 75 a medical check-up has caused some practices problems. Occasionally this work would be undertaken by one of the practice nurses in the patient's home but recently, some practices have managed to get the agreement of district nurses to do the examination opportunistically when visiting their patients to offer other regular treatment. Because of time constraints however, most practices invite elderly patients to come to the surgery for a check-up if they are sufficiently mobile.

It is important that practice and community nurses follow certain protocols established by the GPs in the treatment of various chronic conditions such as asthma, diabetes or leg ulcers. This way the patients receive the same message from all the professionals working for the practice.

▲ Question 11: Health visitors

The GPs in my practice are concerned that the health visitors only manage to visit the mothers of new babies and deal with the problems of the under-fives. How can we persuade them to undertake work with the elderly patients on our list?

Health visitors (HVs) are trained nurses with a post-registration qualification. The GPs do not employ the health visitors directly and so it is usually not possible for them to have any direct control over what the HVs do. On the other hand, the HV's job should be wider than just concentrating on babies and pre-school children – their main remit is to promote health and to this end they have a role in health education and the prevention of disease.

HVs are therefore concerned with promoting the health of all age groups but have a special responsibility for the under-fives. They have to abide by very strict statutory guidelines as to how and when they do the necessary developmental checks on infants and will also try to persuade mothers of the importance of having their baby immunized. Most HVs are also involved in the child health surveillance programmes which GPs undertake.

If there are an above-average number of under-fives on the patient list, or if the practice has insufficient HV hours allocated to them, then the likelihood is that the HVs will be unable to undertake more general health promotion work such as running stress-relief or pre-retirement classes for older patients. Fundholding practices, because they hold their own budgets and purchase the health visiting service, are able to apply pressure on the HVs' employers (usually a local NHS trust) to increase the number of staff allocated to the practice. Alternatively, they might ask the HVs to change their performance to include some of the other health promotion activities they wish to have in their practice.

Non-fundholding practices may find it more difficult to negotiate with the HVs' employer but it should be possible to discuss with the HVs ways in which they themselves might wish to change their working practices. Although many HVs spend a great deal of their time visiting the under-fives in their own homes, they might be prepared to reduce these visits. While it is desirable to see the client's home circumstances on the first occasion, most HVs feel that it is probably not necessary to go to the patient's home on follow-up visits. If the practice can make a room available at the surgery for a regular mother and toddler clinic, not only will the HVs be able to see many more children in a given time but the mothers will also be able to meet, offer support to each other and compare notes. The HVs might also encourage mothers to telephone during the clinic with any queries they might have about their small children.

If the GPs meet the HVs to discuss how they might improve the service and the ways in which the practice can offer more support, you might be surprised by the reaction of the staff concerned. The HVs may be glad to add some diversity to their work and not have to concentrate all their efforts on the under-fives.

▲ Question 12: Midwives

The midwife attached to our practice is not popular with the GPs. She is telling mothers-to-be that they do not need to go to hospital to have their babies and can elect to have them at home if they so wish. The GPs do not want to be responsible for home deliveries as not all of them are obstetrically qualified and for most it is a long time since they last delivered a baby. How can we persuade the midwife to influence mothers to choose hospital as the right place to have their baby?

You can't. Midwives are professionals in their own right and are qualified to undertake deliveries, even in the patient's home, without the assistance of a GP. They will naturally encourage mothers to choose a hospital delivery, if from their medical record it would seem that the mother or baby might be at risk. However, as long as the patient is informed that her GP is not going to be present, unless an emergency arises, there is no good reason why she cannot elect to have her baby at home under the care of the team of midwives.

GPs are not obliged to accept a patient for maternity services who wishes to have a home delivery. The patient can remain on the doctor's list for all other care but sign up with another GP who is willing to offer maternity services including home delivery of the baby. The midwife will naturally be involved not only in the antenatal preparations but also will undertake the immediate postpartum care of mothers and babies.

▲ Question 13: Community psychiatric nurses

I have heard the doctors referring patients to the CPN. Just what does this stand for and what role do they play in the practice?

The CPNs are community psychiatric nurses who have undergone specialist training in the care of patients with mental health problems. They are independent clinical practitioners but are likely to be part of a larger team which may include a consultant psychiatrist and psychologist. They liaise closely with the GPs and take responsibility for care of patients in the community who are mentally ill.

With the introduction of Care in the Community and the subsequent closure of many of the large psychiatric institutions, an increasing number of patients who suffer from some form of mental illness are being treated outside hospital in their own homes. This has increased the workload for CPNs and their role has become crucial in the treatment and care of such patients.

In order to encourage inter-disciplinary liaison, it is helpful if the CPNs are included in any primary health care team meetings. These could be held quarterly, or perhaps only annually, but it is vital that all members of the team occasionally meet to exchange notes and be kept abreast of any developments in the practice.

▲ Question 14: Managers

I am the only manager in our practice and I know of other practices that have different management structures. Can you tell me the ways in which I can share the management responsibility within our practice that might be appropriate for a medium-sized practice of five doctors and 9500 patients?

You are right that some practices have more than one manager. The way in which management responsibilities are allocated will depend very much on the size of practice and the services that are offered. For instance, there are many large practices that have one or more of the following managers in addition to their practice manager.

- business manager
- fundholding manager
- reception manager
- office manager
- practice administrator
- nurse manager
- computer manager.

In a medium-sized practice you will probably need the support of at least one other person in taking responsibility for some aspect of the practice management. She might be subordinate to the practice manager and could be titled deputy manager or assistant practice manager. She should be able to take on some of the day-to-day administrative tasks leaving the practice manager to deal with strategic planning.

In practices of this size or larger there is likely to be a team of three or four practice nurses, some of whom will be working part-time. It makes sense that one of their number should co-ordinate their activities, act as team leader, arrange rotas, liaise with the doctors and health authority, allocate specific tasks among the team and so on. Giving the title of 'nurse manager' to the chosen nurse is not crucial and can cause a problem for the others, who may be equally experienced. However, recognition of the extra work the lead nurse has taken on will be necessary, perhaps by way of a salary increment or re-grading depending on the size of the practice and scope of their additional responsibilities.

Another option, particularly for fundholding practices, is to have a business manager who would work alongside a reception manager and they could split the responsibilities thus:

Business manager	**Reception manager**
Finances	Personnel
Partnership agreement issues	Staff appraisals
Premises	Patient services
Fundholding	Rotas
Liaison with practice accountant and solicitor	Admin systems

There is no right way to establish a management structure in your practice. It will depend on the staff you have at the time, their qualifications and relevant experience, the amount of support given by the partners and your own ability to manage. Each practice will seek its own solution but you should always be ready to re-consider the structure you have in place when the time comes to replace a member of staff. Re-allocating responsibility for various tasks among existing staff can allow for radical change in the management structure should it be required.

▲ Question 15: Medical secretaries

*We have three doctors in the partnership, and three of our five recep-
tionists also each act as secretary to one of the GPs. This means that
there is a problem when a 'secretary' is absent and the particular
doctor wants to dictate referral letters. What can we do to remedy
this?*

The skills required for medical secretarial work, which include
audio-typing of referral letters, are very different from those
required for a medical practice receptionist. It would therefore
seem to be far more efficient to separate the roles and designate
one member of staff to undertake all the secretarial work in the
practice. She would need to have particular expertise in keyboard
skills and be conversant with the medical terminology. In addition
to typing, she could also take calls from patients regarding outpatient referrals and perhaps take on additional administrative
responsibilities such as taking charge of the petty cash, monitoring
fee payments from solicitors for medical reports and so on. If
required she could also be asked to help out in reception on
occasions but I feel strongly that the two roles should be kept
entirely separate if at all possible.

Obviously you will need to provide cover for the secretary
during periods of holiday or sick leave but this should be possible
by designating another member of staff as 'deputy' or by
employing a temporary medical secretary. There might be a
qualified medical secretary in your practice area who has recently
retired and would be willing to do the occasional morning's work.
Alternatively, a young mother, similarly qualified but tied with
small children for most of the time, might be able to make
arrangements to cover when required.

Before you make any such changes, you will need to consult
fully both with the doctors and the staff. In particular you will
need the agreement and support of the receptionists to the idea,
otherwise there is a danger of them feeling demoted and therefore

disenchanted. Other responsibilities could perhaps be allocated to them to 'enrich' their jobs and perhaps the individual receptionists could still take messages for a specific partner to retain some of the 'special relationship'.

▲ Question 16: Receptionists

When I joined the practice we had five full-time receptionists. If one were to fall sick when another was away on holiday it would be difficult for the rest of the team to cope. What is the best way of reducing our dependency on these full-timers?

It is difficult to make immediate changes but the first thing I would do is bring the team of five together and discuss the problem – they might have suggestions to make which could ease the pressure. For instance, you might find that some would be willing to reduce their hours so that one or more part-timers could be employed to allow more flexibility. These new staff would then be expected to do extra hours when required as part of their contract of employment.

You could also seek greater flexibility in the existing staff's working hours in the hope that in quieter times staff would be willing to take time off and then offer to cover at other times when it is busy and they would normally not be working. If no one is willing to do that, you may have to wait until one leaves and then hope to replace them with two part-timers.

Some practices have found that employing part-time staff just to cover the quieter evening surgeries or the emergency Saturday morning surgery can work well. This is particularly so if you always have two staff (for security or other reasons) on duty at any one time. One of the staff could be a permanent full-timer and the other perhaps a part-time evening-only youngster.

In the meantime you should be looking at your procedures in reception to see if there is any way in which the staff's workload could be lightened during busy times. Are the doctors and nurses aware of the problem? Could they reduce their demands on the receptionists at times of crisis? Are the GPs constantly phoning reception to ask for replacement claim forms or other stationery? If so make sure a member of staff is responsible for replenishing these daily in all the consulting rooms. Can the problem of telephone answering be more efficiently undertaken? Are staff spending too long on individual calls? Would training in how to foreshorten calls from patients who are inclined to ramble be helpful? Would the introduction of a computerized appointment system help matters?

All of the above are ways of exploring the problem. There is seldom just one possible solution to a problem and if you learn to think laterally you will be amazed at some of the more unusual alternative solutions you can come up with.

▲ Question 17: Complementary therapists

We would like to offer patients alternative treatments at the surgery. The doctors are particularly keen on providing acupuncture and homeopathy. How do we go about this?

Many practices are now offering the services of a variety of other specialists under the one roof. In many instances, fundholding has enabled practices to do this with health authority agreement. The practice can often pay an outside practitioner a fee from the hospital services element of their budget to cover a regular clinic held at the surgery. The GPs can in turn make a small charge from the complementary therapist to cover the cost of light, heat and reception time in making appointments. The patients are referred by the GPs to the practitioner and can see him or her free of charge. Another possible benefit is that some treatments, if successful, mean that the patient is less likely to require expensive medication and therefore a saving in the practice drugs budget can result.

For practices which do not have a budget, the GPs themselves occasionally decide to offer the additional service of acupuncture or homeopathy if they have the necessary expertise. However, they are not permitted to charge their own patients for the treatment. This can make it an expensive option for the practice, particularly since a homeopathic consultation can last an hour. On the other hand, some practices offer a room to an alternative therapist and then refer patients to them privately, with the patient paying the fee set by the therapist.

▲ Question 18: Counsellor

We employ a counsellor in our practice to whom the GPs refer patients. However, many of the patients do not attend for their appointments and do not let the counsellor know in advance. This can mean an hour is wasted and as there is a waiting list, this seems unfair on everyone concerned. Have you any idea what we can do to improve matters?

This is a not uncommon problem with counselling. Because of the circumstances that have brought patients to seek counselling – perhaps following a bereavement, divorce or enforced redundancy – it is not surprising that they occasionally fail to turn up for appointments.

However, sometimes the fault can lie with inappropriate referrals. There is a temptation for doctors to refer patients who are particularly needy, who consult them frequently and inappropriately without a discernible physical complaint. The patient may not welcome being 'foisted' on to a counsellor and see it as a rejection by their GP. The doctors will need to agree with the counsellor the sort of patients who will benefit from counselling, and who will be likely to attend for their appointments. They will also need to discuss with their patient a possible referral to the counsellor, stressing the need to attend regularly and seeking the patient's full agreement to this as a condition of the referral.

It has also been found that patients who are asked to contribute to the cost of their counselling sessions, are far more likely to keep the appointments and derive benefit from the process. In these circumstances it should be possible for fundholding practices to pay the counsellor a retainer from the budget and allow them to charge the client top-up fees in addition to this retainer. The exact contribution can be negotiated individually with the client according to their means. If the practice is non-fundholding, the client can be charged the full fee or the doctors may decide to subsidise the service from practice funds for those who cannot afford to pay in full. It can be helpful to ask the patient to pay in advance for a number of sessions as this can also ensure better attendance.

▲ Question 19: Community pharmacist

I've read various articles in the GP newspapers stressing the importance of the local pharmacist to doctors. Our practice is in a small town where there is only one chemist but we don't seem to have much contact with him, other than when a problem arises with a prescription. What could we do to improve things?

The role of the community pharmacist has been highlighted in recent years because of the increased pressure on drug budgets. Even practices who are not fundholding have been encouraged by their health authority to reduce their prescribing costs and a trained pharmacist can assist in identifying ways in which this can be achieved. In order to reduce costs, the GPs need to know which treatments are less expensive but still as effective as the dearer equivalents. In some cases a pharmacist can advise on treatments which seem more expensive initially, but which are only required for a limited period of time and so can work out cheaper in the long-term.

On many occasions the local chemist is the first person that a patient contacts for advice about a minor ailment. The pharmacist is almost always available without an appointment and he is likely to have a wide knowledge of drugs and their effectiveness. Pharmacists are trained to educate and counsel patients and can advise on the timing of drugs, the right technique for using an inhaler and the most effective way of applying certain creams or ointments.

In an article published in *Practice Manager*, I identified several benefits that a community pharmacist can provide:[2]

- a prescription collection service
- advice for GPs on setting up a practice formulary
- advice on rationalization of prescribing, e.g. protocols for antibiotics
- medication review for elderly patients.

The medication review can be particularly helpful. Local pharmacists, with GP backing, can encourage elderly customers to bring in for review all the medication they are currently taking, including over-the-counter medicines (OTCs). Elderly patients often hoard half-empty bottles of pills, 'just in case', and overlook the fact that the drugs may be out-of-date, or worse, inappropriate. The pharmacist can review all the medication, check for compliance and contra-indications, advise on possible side-effects and refer the patient back to their GP if necessary.

Perhaps the GPs might like to consider inviting the pharmacist to the next meeting at which they plan to discuss their practice formulary. This can present a potential problem in an area where there is more than one chemist, as GPs cannot be seen to be favouring one over another. However, even in areas where there are several pharmacists, there is no reason why they cannot band together to discuss jointly with the GPs ways in which they can be of mutual help. It seems a shame to have the potential resource of a professional with such valuable expertise and not fully utilize this for the benefit of the practice and the patients.

▲ Question 20: Patients

The partners are adamant that they will not countenance a patient participation group (PPG) at this practice. I think they fear that a vocal group of patients could attempt to start dictating to the GPs certain changes in the services offered at the surgery. What can I say to make the doctors change their minds because I think a PPG could be a great idea?

First, we should define just what a patient participation group is. It is usually a group of patients who, with the encouragement of the GPs in a particular practice, offer support to the practice and to the community. Services which such groups sometimes perform include:

- a repeat prescription collection service for housebound patients
- transport to and from the surgery or local hospital outpatients department for patients who do not have their own transport
- useful feedback, not always adverse criticism, on matters of concern raised by individual patients
- 'befriending' service for elderly or disabled patients
- fundraising for specialist clinical equipment for the surgery.

If the PPG is a registered charity, then any equipment bought with donated funds will remain the property of the charity but can be given on permanent loan to the practice.

The doctors themselves need not have a great deal of contact with the group which should allay their fears of becoming involved in a lot of lengthy meetings with irate patients berating them. The group can be organized by the patients themselves with the practice manager acting as liaison person within the practice. Some groups employ a paid co-ordinator to manage the volunteers who run the transport schemes and organize fundraising activities. In my experience, PPGs are a definite bonus and a potential resource for the GPs to call on rather than a drain. They should be encouraged.

▲ Question 21: Personal lists

Two of the partners in our practice have decided to reduce their full-time commitment, and job-share instead. This will mean taking on a new partner. How can we re-allocate the patients registered with the original partners fairly in the new arrangement?

There is no simple answer to this dilemma as several practices have found to their cost. One practice I know chose to divide the current lists in half alphabetically, leaving 50% of the patients of each half-time GP registered with their original doctor, and the remaining patients allocated to the new partner. This meant that Dr A's patients with surnames beginning A–M would be on the list of the job-sharing partners (thus still being able to see Dr A at least half the time) but patients with names from N–Z would be allocated to the new doctor, Dr C. Likewise, patients N–Z for Dr B would be on the job-sharers' list, and the A–M patients would be allocated to Dr C. This proved to be a very unpopular division since the patients who were no longer able to see their own GP naturally felt angry when they discovered that their neighbour, who had also previously been on the list, was still able to see the doctor while they could not just because their name began with the wrong initial letter. Obviously, this method is not to be recommended.

Another possible way of doing it would be to say that all Dr A's patients would remain on the job-sharers' list, and Dr B's patients would then be moved to the list of the new doctor, Dr C. Again Dr B's patients might not be pleased that while their doctor was still practising, they were unable to consult him.

If the doctors do not keep strict personal lists, then it is far less of a problem. All patients can make an appointment with whichever doctor they wish to see. The availability of the individual job-sharers would be halved, so patients would find it more difficult to get an urgent appointment with either of them and therefore be prepared to see the new doctor. Much of course will depend on the character and reputation of all the doctors involved, but given time a suitable balance will generally be found.

2

Managing

Managerial effectiveness is a crucial element in the running of any business and this concept can be defined as 'the extent to which a manager achieves intended objectives'. In order to manage a general practice you will require a number of management skills, many of them related to man-management. However, you will also need to know how to adapt to change, plan for the future and enable the GPs to do the same.

The following questions and answers will cover many of the more obvious skills such as team-building, leadership, motivating staff, time management, decision-making and planning. Just because general practice is not a commercial business does not mean that you do not have to be business-like in your approach. In fact the opposite is true. Because general practice is part of the NHS, there is an even greater requirement for sound management and accountability.

The patients have the right to a good level of service from their GP surgery and the GPs themselves deserve an adequate level of remuneration for providing such a service. To satisfy these two needs, both the staff and the complicated finances of the business will need to be managed expertly and it will not be sufficient merely to try and maintain the status quo as everything around you changes. If you are to keep ahead of the field you will need to plan for the future and constantly be looking for ways of improving the services you offer.

The financial management of the practice will be covered in the second book in *The Practice Manager Library*. Issues relating to cashflow projections, spreadsheets, bank reconciliations, reimbursements, budgeting and stock control will all be addressed, so this section will concentrate solely on the management of people and systems.

Many of the questions in this section are subsumed under headings of wider management issues such as planning, delegating and team-building. However, all the replies offer solutions to management problems directly relating to, and experienced in, general practice. The specific problems experienced by those managers who have worked in the practice before in a different capacity and are trying to adjust to their new role will also be touched on. It can be very hard to gain acceptance as a manager, both from the GPs and the staff, when you have previously worked as a receptionist or secretary in the same practice.

▲ Question 22: Team-building

The doctors come to work each day, see 20 patients in surgery and then leave. They don't seem to want to be involved in the general running of the practice. How can I persuade everyone to work better as a team?

A woman GP once told me that the reason why she had chosen to work in general practice, rather than hospital medicine, was because she preferred to work as an individual independent contractor. The idea of working in a team was anathema to her. This applies to many GPs to whom the concept of team-working is entirely alien.

However, with the increasing emphasis on primary care,

practices are expanding to include other professionals offering care to patients. Physiotherapists and chiropodists, complementary therapists such as acupuncturists and osteopaths are all now working within practices. It is also evident that even non-clinical staff are making an indirect contribution to the effective treatment of patients, and thus are also essential members of the team. The GPs have to accept that, whether they like it or not, they are part of a growing team working in primary health care and they will need to recognize this if they are to provide a comprehensive and cohesive service to their patients.

A team will need a leader and if none of the partners is willing to take on this role then the most appropriate person may be you as practice manager. Part of your job should include learning about each individual, their strengths and weaknesses, their goals and hopes. You will need to work out how everyone fits into the team and then facilitate each member working to his or her best ability. This applies not only to the staff but also to the GPs.

Every team needs people with complementary skills. Belbin identified eight distinct personality types which a good team should include.[3] Some people will be able to play more than one role but to have a balanced team it is important to try and incorporate as many of the following types as possible:

- **The company worker** – conservative, practical, methodical, trustworthy, predictable and hard-working
- **The chairman** – controlled, disciplined, strong sense of objectives, good judge of people, able to welcome potential contributors without prejudice
- **The shaper** – dynamic, outgoing, dominant, challenges inertia and complacency
- **The plant** – individualistic, intellectually dominant, imaginative and knowledgeable
- **The resource investigator** – extrovert, popular, communicative, responds to challenges
- **The monitor–evaluator** – unemotional, analytical, discreet, hard-headed

- **The team-worker** – sociable, supportive, sensitive, promotes team spirit
- **The completer–finisher** – painstaking, conscientious, capacity for follow-through.

Imagine a team without a plant who will think up the ideas and have the energy to introduce them. And without a completer–finisher these ideas will never become firm courses of action followed through to the end. When recruiting staff, or choosing a new partner, it is important to identify the strengths and weaknesses of existing members and try to determine which particular skills and personal characteristics are required to complement your team.

The benefits of good team-working are many but one of the main advantages must be the support that staff and doctors can give each other, particularly when they are able to appreciate the work being done by all the members of the team. If there are colleagues who understand the work of others and can appreciate just what it involves, the practice will not become overly dependent on any one individual. Others can step in to take over during an absence.

Staff bring with them experiences and skills that can be of benefit to the whole team. Teams have the facility to build upon these various skills and the different ideas which individuals can produce. If good team-working is achieved, a shared sense of purpose will result and this will in turn generate a more motivated staff, a less stressed group of GPs and more contented patients. That has to be a worthwhile goal to work towards.

▲ Question 23: Leadership

No one seems to be in charge at the practice. No one will take responsibility for anything. The GPs pass all problems on to me and the staff do likewise. How can I get them to take some responsibility themselves?

There is a definite need for leadership skills in the running of any business. In general practice it will almost certainly be the practice manager who has to supply these. You will need to be goal-orientated, self-motivated and possess boundless energy and have to learn how to exert influence effectively in all directions – upwards, downwards and sideways. You will need to show strong leadership both to the partners and the staff but it will naturally be evidenced in different ways.

A democratic style of leadership is the one most likely to work in the culture of general practice as a more dictatorial approach can alienate all the members of the team. Therefore, you will need to listen to what people tell you and help them to find possible solutions themselves to the problems they raise – you will have to act as facilitator to make this come about. If someone has had a hand in reaching a decision on a course of action, rather than having it imposed on them, then they are more likely to work towards a successful outcome.

In order to influence the GPs, you will need to earn their respect and hope to be perceived as both credible and reliable. They will want to see evidence of your ability to analyze problems and present plausible solutions. You will also need to be seen to be fair, treating each partner equally and never showing any sign of favouritism. This is harder than it sounds at times since there are bound to be one or two of the partners whom you find it easier to work with than others.

Strict neutrality is also necessary in your dealings with the staff. It is difficult to maintain a strictly unbiased approach if you are particularly friendly with one or more members of staff. This need for impartiality means that the job of practice manager can be lonely (*see* Questions **50** and **51** on isolation and networking).

▲ Question 24: Away day

Partners' meetings in our practice are always acrimonious. The doctors never seem to agree on anything and are always changing their minds. If plans are agreed, they are invariably rescinded before they have had a chance to become established. What can I do?

It is not uncommon for GPs to disagree. Many doctors chose to work in general practice because they liked the idea of being an 'independent contractor' rather than having to work in the hierarchy which exists in hospitals. Thus GPs can become resentful that they have been forced by the economies of scale, and the encouragement of the DoH, to form partnerships in order to offer a more comprehensive and cost-effective service to patients. Team-working is therefore not something that necessarily comes easily to the average GP.

One way of establishing some ground rules is to plan an 'away day' when the partners can take time out from the pressures of the practice to talk to each other in depth about their hopes for the future of the practice. It is vital that an agenda is set for the day, with a list of subjects that need to be discussed. This should be adhered to and no deviations permitted – which is easier said than done.

The first requirement will be to find a suitable date. A weekend is ideal since locum cover will be less expensive than during the week. The venue should be chosen at sufficient distance from the practice to ensure anonymity and confidentiality, but close enough not to necessitate time-consuming travel arrangements. It is a bonus if there are leisure facilities at the place selected so that a break can be taken at some stage during the day to enable everyone to swim, play tennis or just have a meal together.

Having chosen your date and venue, you will now need to decide who will facilitate the day. As manager, you could undertake this role yourself if you feel confident enough of your ability to do this difficult but essential task. Alternatively you could hire someone from outside the practice who can provide a neutral, objective view of the proceedings. You might want to invite a GP from another practice, a manager working in the health authority or perhaps a psychologist experienced in facilitating such events. The chosen facilitator should ensure that everyone's views are taken into account and that discussions never become too heated. The facilitator should also lead the group towards consensus whenever possible and make sure that agreement is eventually reached.

Following a successful away day I organized for a partnership of six GPs, at which the chief executive of a health authority (previously unknown to the partners) acted as facilitator, the remark was made by one of the doctors, 'Well that went well. We didn't really need the facilitator did we?' The facilitator had done his job so well and so unobtrusively that his presence was deemed to have been unnecessary. Without him it could have been disastrous. There is a danger of matters being raised that are not adequately resolved and this in turn can lead to unfulfilled expectations and subsequent disappointments.

Prior to the meeting it is often advisable to do a SWOT analysis of the practice (*see* Question **41**). This management jargon, if you have not come across it, is an acronym for **s**trengths, **w**eaknesses, **o**pportunities and **t**hreats. The analysis, if undertaken properly, should help you to identify what is happening in the practice under these headings and it should provide a useful basis for your discussions.

You will need to arrange for someone to record the agreements made during the day and it may be appropriate if you, as practice manager, undertake the minute-taking to ensure confidentiality. Following the away day, it is obviously essential that any plans made are implemented and you will play a major part in ensuring that this happens and that agreements are honoured. Some of the plans discussed may be for long-term development in the practice and you will need to prepare an appropriate feasibility study or plan in order to carry the proposed project forward.

An away day such as this can provide a forum for the partners to talk to each other about where they hope to be in five years, and how they envisage the future of the practice. The doctors will be able to talk at length about their individual hopes and plans. A doctor close to retirement might state that he hopes to reduce his out-of-hours commitment to allow him more time to spend pursuing leisure activities. Another might declare his intention of taking a sabbatical in three years' time in order to travel abroad and practise medicine in a different environment. A partner might state that her objective is to job-share at some time in the near future because of family commitments and she might welcome her partners' agreement in principle to this idea and support for it when the time comes.

Following such a day spent together in discussion, it can be apparent that the doctors have gained a far better understanding of the needs and aspirations of their partners and are prepared to accommodate them as far as possible both now and in the future. A strategic plan for the practice as a whole for the next five years, based on these preliminary discussions, should result. This can then be used as a foundation for many new projects introduced over the years.

▲ Question 25: Planning

We seem to stagger from crisis to crisis in our practice and no one has any idea what they are meant to be doing. Any suggestions as to how I can bring some element of order to the practice?

One of the most important aspects of effective management is good planning. In the past, when few practices employed managers, there was no particular person whose job it was to give the partners and staff a sense of direction. The GPs were too busy treating patients to have time to look ahead and decide how they could best prepare for the future development of their practice.

Planning need not be difficult and simply requires time and

thought. You probably had a plan in mind when you sat down to read this. You may have a pencil and notepad to hand, made sure that there would be no telephone interruptions and chosen a time and place when you could be assured of peace and quiet to enable you to concentrate. Even if you are reading in the bath, these factors still apply.

Planning can vary in scale from the relative simplicity of planning a meeting to the mammoth task of planning the development of the practice including new premises, an additional partner and recruitment of more staff. Planning is a process and can be complex. Frequently, the planning process is interrupted and confused by the messy and iterative steps that are required to complete the plan.

Once you have established what it is you need to do, you will have to decide just how to go about doing it. That done, you will need to determine just what steps will be required in order to achieve the desired ends. When you have drawn up your preliminary plan, a review might be a good idea. Is it going to work? If not, try going back one or two steps and adjusting your plan.

So that is planning in a nutshell. But where to start in a muddled practice? Well you might want to do an analysis of the practices' strengths and weaknesses (*see* Question **41** on SWOT analysis) which could be followed by an away day (*see* Question **24**). The results of such analysis and discussion can lead to the production of a strategic plan. This might be on the subject of how to cope with premises that are too constrictive for all the additional services that are being devolved to primary care. Or the plan could be on ways to reward the staff for working under particularly difficult conditions during building renovations. Whatever the problem, it will help everyone to feel less rudderless and more purposeful if careful preparation has gone into the making-up of the final plan.

Once the strategic plan is drawn up, an operational plan can follow. This is likely to deal in detail with the specific objectives that have been identified and the timescale involved in achieving each step which will ultimately lead to the desired goal.

A last thought – do not forget that you might need a contingency plan for when everything goes wrong and your original strategy goes awry.

▲ Question 26: Staff recruitment

One of our young receptionists is leaving soon and we need to replace her. Do we have to go through the expensive business of advertising, short-listing and interviewing or can we just ask our existing members of staff to put the word about that we are looking for a receptionist?

It can be very time-consuming to go through the normal recruitment process and whether you decide to do this or not will depend very much on where your practice is located and what the chances are of recruiting successfully by word-of-mouth. If your practice is small and rural it may seem easier just to ask around because everyone is likely to know everyone else in the community. Reception work in general practice is still considered to be an enviable and enjoyable job for many women who have few qualifications. If I were a cynic, I might suggest that this is because they have had little first-hand experience of the reality of working in a busy surgery.

A GP receptionist will need to have good communication skills, a thick skin, an equable temperament, the ability to work well in a team and will require a basic knowledge of computers and databases. The chosen candidate will also have to fit into the existing team.

One danger with recruiting by word-of-mouth is that you may find yourself reluctant to take up references. Or perhaps you will find it difficult to turn down a person recommended by an existing member of staff, even though you believe that they are not really suitable for the job. There is also the possibility of cliques forming within a small team if two members of the staff are close friends. Others can feel excluded and resentful and this can be exacerbated if the new member of staff is also a personal friend of one of the doctors.

Once you have determined just what the job description should include, you will be able to list the qualities you require in the successful applicant. These might include basic qualifications such as keyboard skills and computer literacy and experience of filing and working with the public. You should then draw up the person specification including all these requirements. An advertisement in a local paper need not be expensive and the local job centre will always welcome details of any vacancy. They will usually be prepared to filter applicants, sending only those who fulfil the criteria you have stipulated.

You can then compare all the applications to your person speci-fication and easily weed out those who do not have the necessary qualifications and experience that you have specified. Do not overlook the need to achieve complementarity within the team if possible. It is important that you include people with different skills and temperaments which together help to create a complete team. It is not generally advisable to choose people who are too similar and expect them to work closely together.

One of the partners may wish to interview with you, and the other doctors might insist on meeting the short-listed candidates too. It is particularly helpful if each of the candidates is introduced to the reception team and spends time (prior to or following their interview) talking to the other receptionists. This can also provide an opportunity for the applicants to be shown around the practice to see for themselves the conditions in which they will be working.

The staff will have their own views on which of the candidates they feel they could or could not work with. If you choose a candidate without taking into account any negative views expressed by other members of the team, you may find the staff unwilling to offer adequate support to the new employee during the induction period and the whole appointment will be doomed to failure.

▲ Question 27: Staff appraisals

I have recently been appointed as practice manager in a small rural practice where previously one of the partners acted as manager on one half-day per week. I have discovered that there are no personnel files for members of staff and no record of any appraisals. When I suggested that I wished to introduce staff appraisals the doctors were sceptical of the effectiveness of such a course, and the staff admitted they felt threatened by the idea. Can you suggest ways in which I can persuade both the GPs and the staff of the necessity for regular appraisals?

You are not alone in working in a practice that has no experience of staff appraisals. The first thing you will need to do is explain to the partners the advantages that regular appraisals can bring to the practice. Appraisals should not be about pointing out bad working practices and punishing poor workers. Rather they provide an opportunity for the appraiser and individual staff members to establish goals and specific objectives for a given timescale, usually the year ahead.

The appraisal interview should provide a forum for feedback from the employee as well as a chance for the manager to praise past efforts and offer constructive criticism on ways in which improvements can take place. Training needs can be identified and methods of monitoring development can be set up.

If you explain to staff that one of the reasons why you wish to hold individual appraisals is because you wish to learn from them how they feel about their particular job and their role in the practice, this should ensure that they begin to feel less apprehensive about the whole process. You will need to discover what they think about their working conditions, whether they enjoy the work, how they feel that it might be improved or made easier and changes that they believe would be advantageous. It is obviously important that you listen to their views and recommendations and, where possible, implement changes that they have suggested.

At one practice, I made a point of talking at length to each member of staff individually within the first week following my appointment. This gave me the opportunity to learn what was of particular importance to each person, what changes they would like to see made and how they saw their future and that of the practice. All three of the practice nurses mentioned that their treatment room needed a new floor and suggested that the glass door should be replaced with a solid one to ensure privacy for patients. I persuaded the GPs that a new floor was indeed essential for reasons of hygiene and we replaced the existing one with an inexpensive but safe vinyl covering. We compromised on the door by using a semi-opaque film which was placed over the glass to restrict visibility but still allow light through. The nurses were happy with this and acknowledged that I had indeed proved that I could get things done as promised. Thereafter they were more prepared to discuss further changes that the GPs wanted them to make in other areas.

A comment made by several of the receptionists during their appraisal was that they particularly disliked the endless filing and pulling of notes which they were currently expected to do. Following this, I managed to persuade the GPs that by employing a part-time filing clerk, we could release the more highly paid receptionists to do income-generating tasks such as completing and checking items-of-service claims. This meant that the receptionists were able to incorporate more interesting tasks into their work and no longer felt burdened by the tedium of filing. Incidentally, it also had the effect of introducing an amazing individual to the practice who took sole responsibility for the filing of all medical records. She managed to eliminate the problem of missing notes almost entirely by ensuring that a foolproof system of tracers was used at all times.

Appraisals need not always be undertaken by a superior of subordinates. There is also upward appraisal where a manager lays herself open to assessment by the staff with whom she works. This can prove very revealing but will need to be managed with care if it is not to degenerate merely into an opportunity for destructive criticism and the settling of old scores.

There is also something to be said for peer review by the GPs. This is a form of appraisal of each other which they could undertake at regular intervals. Many doctors are very protective of their right to practise medicine in their own way and thus find it threatening to have to accept criticism from their partners. However, they should be able to discuss matters such as prescribing within a previously agreed formulary, or treating patients with chronic conditions such as asthma or diabetes to an agreed protocol. This peer review would enable each of them to listen to the others' views and aspirations, comment on working practices, discuss areas of potential conflict and resolve any difficulties in a protected environment.

Without regular appraisals it is difficult to form a coherent plan of where the practice is going and how the staff are expected to develop. A business that stands still will soon begin to go backwards. We all need to move forwards and it helps if all the staff are behind you and willing to work to the agreed goals.

For a detailed analysis of how to go about setting up a staff appraisal system, see the chapter on *How to appraise staff* in Irvine and Haman.[4]

▲ Question 28: Motivating staff

It seems to me that one of the most important aspects of my job is to try to keep both the GPs and staff happy. How can I help the receptionists to work well in their often thankless task of trying to please both patients and doctors, and at the same time find job satisfaction themselves?

Motivating staff is an essential part of any manager's work. Tyson and York define motivation as 'an inner force that impels human beings to behave in a variety of ways'.[5] They also give brief details of the theories of some authors who have undertaken research studies into motivation, e.g. Maslow, Herzberg, McGregor, Mayo and others. You will come across the work of these people in most books on management.

In general practice, as elsewhere, it is no longer sufficient just to offer a job, pay an agreed salary and expect the employee to be happy. Irvine and Haman admit that 'recognizing and addressing the fact that people's knowledge, skills, capabilities, motivation and value do not develop automatically is a crucial management skill.'[4]

A full contract of employment is the first step in ensuring that the individual knows just what conditions to expect in their work. A comprehensive job description and regular appraisals should follow. However, the whole process of assessment and support has to develop progressively so that the individual continues to feel a valued member of the team. Most employees seek not only an interesting job but usually like to feel that what they are doing is worthwhile and that they have job security. They need to respect their boss(es) and preferably have some opportunity for advancement or improvement. This latter point is not always easy to achieve in general practice where most receptionists have few career prospects. However, there is no reason why they cannot learn new skills and gain wider experience of all facets of general practice reception work which should help them to feel that they are not simply standing still.

Staff are more likely to be motivated if they receive recognition and praise when it is deserved but giving indiscriminate praise is counter-productive; any commendation should be genuinely earned. The manager is not the only one who can offer praise, however. The GPs, other members of staff and even the patients can all help in making individuals feel valued if they also offer their occasional approval or thanks.

All the staff will work better if the management of the practice is not only consistent but also seen to be fair. People need to have clear objectives and a sense of purpose if they are to work to their best ability and as manager you will be expected to give a firm lead and ensure that everyone knows what is expected of them.

The variety of work within general practice can be a motivating factor for many of the staff and the fact that much of their time will be spent dealing with people (in itself both challenging and rewarding) is often seen as a positive benefit. Staff seem to value a sense of belonging and strong team leadership (*see* Question **23**) can certainly help to achieve this and also foster a spirit of co-operation and mutual support.

Job satisfaction is important and setting achievable goals for individual members of staff is an integral part of enabling them to experience job satisfaction – this can be done during an appraisal (*see* Question **27**). You must recognize, however, that people will have their own goals as well as organizational ones and when the two coincide you are more likely to have a contented and able worker.

▲ Question 29: Job enrichment

I recently heard the expression 'job enrichment' at a management seminar but would welcome an explanation of just what this means.

Job enrichment is a term used to describe changes in work patterns and conditions aimed specifically at increasing the level of responsibility of individual members of staff. However, it should more correctly be reserved for specific programmes of change which relate directly to Herzberg's two-factor theory of job satisfaction. Herzberg classified two categories of needs corresponding to the lower and higher levels of human goals and named one group 'hygiene factors' and the other group 'motivators'. The first are the environmental factors such as working conditions, pay and job security which need constant attention in order to prevent dissatisfaction. The 'motivators' group come from internal sources and the opportunities afforded by the job for self-fulfilment. If a worker finds his job meaningless, he may react apathetically. Herzberg believed that a manager cannot motivate but only stimulate or stifle self-motivation and 'the primary function of any organization... should be to implement the needs of man to enjoy a meaningful existence.'[6] It is certainly evident that if people enjoy their work, they are more likely to work well.

Herzberg suggested that staff would work better if they had more autonomy and were given a complete natural unit of work to complete as opposed to the conveyor belt approach. This is virtually impossible to achieve in general practice where there are so many part-time workers and work is often fragmented and demand-led. However, there are specific tasks for which individuals can take responsibility such as collating temporary resident claims, monitoring maternity forms, maintaining the Warfarin records and entering pathology results on to the computer. If staff take individual responsibility for a specific task they are more likely to achieve satisfaction in their work. Herzberg also suggested that introducing new and more difficult tasks from time to time helps workers to develop and learn new skills. Everyone likes to become a recognized 'expert' and there is no reason why the receptionists should not be encouraged to become 'expert' at one particular aspect of their job.

When you are seeking to enrich the jobs of your subordinates, do not forget to make your own work more interesting. Set yourself the challenge of acquiring new skills, taking on additional tasks which you had previously thought to be beyond your capabilities. Then you too will grow and develop in your work, and will almost certainly end up feeling more fulfilled.

▲ Question 30: Effective delegation

I am seldom able to complete any task that I planned to do during the day because of constant interruptions, often for minor crises in reception. How can I make time for the financial and strategic planning that I know is required if we are not to continue stumbling from crisis to crisis?

If you wish to succeed as a manager you will first need to learn to say 'no' and to do this you will have to learn to delegate effectively which is the essence of good management. Jenks and Kelly assert that 'delegating is a method of fulfilling your responsibilities, not avoiding them.'[7] It is not about dumping unwanted tasks on to subordinates but rather identifying certain jobs that could well be undertaken by another member of staff, releasing you to do more important tasks. You will still remain accountable for the actual task but can reasonably give to others the day-to-day responsibility for many of the jobs often done by the practice manager. In turn this will allow junior staff to develop new skills and experience the satisfaction that comes with assuming additional responsibility.

Some tasks that you might consider delegating, if you have not already done so, might be:

- **control of the petty cash** – you could remain the second signatory on petty cash vouchers and ensure that one person alone is not responsible for the management of money within the practice
- **receptionist duty rotas** – one of the senior receptionists can usefully take on this task once you have discussed the system you want her to use
- **sorting the mail** – a receptionist can sort the GPs' mail into their trays and abstract any invoices, remittances and other papers that the GPs are happy to divert directly to you for action
- **responsibility for stock-control**
- **dealing with patients' enquiries about hospital outpatient appointments** – this can be done equally well by the secretary who types the referral letters
- **ordering treatment room supplies and negotiating discounts on injectables** – this can be done by the nurse clerk if you have one or possibly by one of the practice nurses

- **computer problem solving** – if you can train up one of the
staff with an aptitude for computer work to take responsibility
for solving the inevitable problems that arise with the system,
you will find that they gain a certain expertise which in turn
means that fewer problems arise in the future.

When you have managed to delegate tasks, do not cast adrift the
person to whom you have delegated or leave them unsupervised.
Offer support as required and be available for advice until they are
happy to assume full responsibility. You can then begin to plan
your own time more effectively and get on with the wider view of
strategic planning (*see* Question **33**).

▲ Question 31: Disciplinary matters

*One of our patients complained that he had first learned of his wife's
pregnancy from a member of the practice staff whom he bumped into
in the supermarket. How should I discipline the member of staff
concerned?*

First of all you will need to find out whether the complaint is well-
founded. Talk to the member of staff concerned and find out her
side of the story. She may deny having said anything in which
case, you may have to look for witnesses to the alleged breach of
confidentiality. Did someone overhear their conversation? If you
can get no firm evidence to prove beyond reasonable doubt that
there was a breach of confidence, you may have to inform the
member of staff that you noted on her file that the complaint has
been made but found unproven. However, you must explain that
if there is a similar incident in future and the case against her can
be proved, it will be grounds for instant dismissal. You must, of
course, apologize to the patient and her husband and let them
know that you have taken the matter very seriously and have
accordingly taken the appropriate steps.

If, on the other hand, the member of staff concerned admits that she did indeed congratulate the man, who was well known to her, on his impending fatherhood then this is quite another matter. She might claim, with some justification, that she had automatically assumed that his wife would already have informed him of her pregnancy. You might then feel that this was a genuine, if regrettable, mistake and rather than punishment, the offer of training in how to avoid divulging confidential information might be a more appropriate course of action.

GPs have to deal every day with meeting patients socially about whom they know intimate and confidential facts. They are therefore well-qualified to offer staff training in how to avoid falling into the trap of inadvertently disclosing privileged information about a patient. You could take the opportunity to ask all staff to attend such a training session, given by one of the doctors, on the subject of respecting confidentiality. Without identifying the culprit, you could cite a similar case and demonstrate just how easy it can be to let slip confidential information about a patient. You could use role play to help illustrate the kind of scenario where the staff might experience problems in knowing just how to respond without divulging confidential information. If staff are reminded of the importance of respecting patient confidentiality and given tips on how to avoid being drawn into conversations that can lead to such indiscretions, they will feel more confident in their ability to respect privileged information.

▲ Question 32: Dealing with staff problems

We have a thief in our midst. Small amounts of money have gone missing from the cash float which we keep at reception. Recently a member of our staff lost some money from her handbag which she left under the reception desk. I have a shrewd idea of who the thief might be, but it is virtually impossible to prove anything. What should we do?

Having a thief at work makes everyone feel uneasy – no one likes to leave their possessions lying around and everyone feels under suspicion. Even if the amounts stolen are trivial, as in your case, you cannot ignore the matter and I suggest that you gather all the staff together and explain the situation to them. Point out that money is going missing and that if this continues you will feel bound to call in the police. This will at least have the effect of informing the thief that you know what is going on. You may wish to interview members of staff individually to see if the likely time of the thefts can be determined and, if so, whether there is a pattern which would help to identify the culprit. For instance, if money goes missing when only two members of staff are on duty in the evening, you will at least have narrowed it down.

If the thefts continue, however, you will then have to decide whether to confront the person you believe to be responsible or to call the police. Their uniformed presence on the premises might scare the thief sufficiently to deter them from stealing again. Alternatively, the police might suggest ways in which you could trap the thief by marking banknotes or coins in some way to enable you to identify them. But would you want to ask all the staff to empty their purses to search for marked cash? It is unlikely that the police will be of real help unless you can provide further evidence which might lead to identification of the thief.

You should try to reassure staff that you are taking the matter seriously and at the same time caution them to keep their belongings secure. You could offer to lock any valuables away during working hours, or you might consider providing individual lockers for staff. Unfortunately there is no simple solution to your dilemma. However, an atmosphere of suspicion can be very damaging to staff morale and so it is important to clear matters up as soon as possible one way or another.

▲ Question 33: Time management

I never seem to have enough time to do all the things I want to in the surgery. No sooner do I arrive when I am bombarded with trivial problems which seem to end up occupying me for most of the day. How can I change this and actually make time to manage the practice rather than continue merely to react?

Benjamin Franklin in 1746 said 'Dost thou love life? Then do not squander time for that's the stuff life is made of.' This is relevant to general practice management as in everything else. The first thing you should realize is that it is not only your own time that you will need to manage if you are in charge of a practice. You may also be required to help the GPs to manage their time and, of course, the staff will need your help in planning their time to best effect.

To manage time effectively, you will need to:

* plan
* set up good systems for dealing with potential problems
* delegate effectively
* eliminate time-wasting activities wherever possible.

Other questions in this book deal with detailed planning (*see* Question **25**), including doing a SWOT analysis (*see* Question **41**) and producing a business plan (*see* Question **42**). If you plan well, you will anticipate possible problems and have set-up contingency plans to deal with them. Computer crashes are just such a case and inevitably they come at the most inconvenient moments. If, however, you have good contingency plans and the staff know exactly what they should do, staff can overcome potential problems caused by any breakdown in the computer system fairly quickly.

Setting up a manual system such as a log recording details of equipment maintenance contracts and visits can enable others to access the information when required without having to interrupt you to ask. All practices have equipment, both clinical and office, which need to be maintained: autoclaves, hydraulic couches, fire extinguishers, security and fire systems, fax machines and photocopiers. Without a clear record it is difficult to keep tabs on when they were last serviced. One main log of all the equipment should be accessible to any of the staff and in it should be recorded the name of the company who normally services the machine, the date of previous service visits, the nature of any problems experienced and the solution found to such problems. When something goes wrong staff can then access the log and attempt previous solutions before calling the engineer. The service contract number and details of the make and model of the machine which they can quote will also be available. This all saves time and avoids the situation where staff hunt frantically for details, are unable to find them and end up putting the problem on your desk rather than dealing with the matter themselves.

Other records which are useful to keep in reception are a file detailing all requests for medical insurance reports including the date they arrive in the practice, the date they were despatched and when payment was finally received. This is a simple system that can be administered by one of the reception staff. Any telephone calls relating to insurance reports can then be passed to this one individual if she is available. If she is absent, access to the file should enable anyone to respond appropriately to the caller offering the details required from the written record.

Delegation is dealt with elsewhere in this section (*see* Question **30**). It is one of the most important elements of time management and you should be aware of the necessity for learning to delegate effectively. It will not only release your own time for other projects but will also enable various members of staff to take on more responsibility and gain new skills. For instance, if you are still controlling the petty cash do you really need to be doing this? Could you delegate this to the medical secretary or a senior receptionist? You could still retain overall supervision.

Eliminating time-wasting is another sure way of making more

time for important work. Badly organized meetings are an irritating waste of time and usually end up being counter-productive. Make sure that your meetings are managed as well as possible and that they only last as long as is strictly necessary (*see* Question **45** on meetings). Do not procrastinate. You will need to be disciplined and deal with things in a logical sequence – sort papers in your in-tray as they arrive, rather than handling them several times. If you have an accurate filing system and ensure that you file all papers that have been dealt with as soon as possible, you will save the time often spent searching through piles on your desk. The exact type of filing system adopted does not matter – what does, however, is your ability to retrieve important papers quickly and easily.

Try not to get side-tracked when embarking on any task. A telephone call can easily derail you from the job in hand. Re-route calls when you are dealing with important matters and shut your office door occasionally and make sure you get uninterrupted time to think and plan. Management is not just about frenetic activity, rushing around sorting out crises but it should involve long-term planning of practice development and careful monitoring of the finances of the practice.

When you have released all this time, you will be able to concentrate on managing the practice more efficiently and also help others in the practice to manage their time.

▲ Question 34: Decision-making

How can I get the partners to stick to decisions that they have made? They all get together to discuss an issue, agree a solution and then one or more of them subsequently change their mind.

This is a perennial difficulty in any partnership, the main problem being that you have more than one boss. In a large practice there might be as many as seven or eight employers to whom the manager is accountable and obtaining their agreement for anything, particularly if they insist on consensus, is difficult. Trying to make them all adhere to agreements is even more problematic.

There is probably no such thing as a perfect decision, but your aim should be to enable the partners to reach the best decision they are capable of making in the circumstances and one to which they will stick. In partnerships there is always the problem of several doctors all having equal authority, who almost certainly hold different views on many aspects of running the practice. They will also probably find it difficult to accept and accommodate views that differ from their own. However, as they jointly own the business as partners they have to be encouraged to make sound decisions and then stick to them.

Stewart stresses that a logical sequence of steps should be carried out in reaching a decision.[8] She identified three items:

- the reasons for taking a decision must be formulated, usually by defining a problem that is to be solved. The right questions need to be asked
- the nature of the problem needs to be analyzed
- alternative solutions must be examined, together with any possible ramifications.

She states that 'the correctness of these preliminary stages will have great influence on the validity of the final decisions.'

It is certainly easier to make good decisions if you have available all the relevant information. It is helpful if any research required is done beforehand and all the partners have the appropriate papers to read in advance of the meeting. Asking the right questions can help everyone to define the problem accurately – solutions that might work can then be sought and any possible unwanted side-effects identified. The partners will then be better informed and, it is hoped, feel better able to make a sound decision.

The rational approach to decision-making requires that you go through a sequence of steps in a logical and systematic way, enabling you to take every relevance into account and give due weight to all possible considerations. You will be expected to:

- analyze and define the problem
- set the objectives
- obtain all relevant information
- seek as many potential solutions and reasonable alternatives as possible
- evaluate each solution
- choose the solution which best matches the criteria you have established
- take appropriate action.

If this all seems rather obvious it is often the case that these logical steps are not taken when important decisions are being made and explains why the proposed solution frequently proves to be unworkable. It is also essential to remember to go back through some of the steps again if the chosen solution does not prove satisfactory. This will enable you to find an alternative which might be more successful.

The Industrial Society identifies the following steps in taking a decision which are not dissimilar from those listed above under the rational approach:

- **consider** – identify the actual problem
- **clarify** – check for cause and effect
- **consult** – call a meeting to obtain maximum amount of information
- **crunch** – gather all the options and take the decision
- **communicate** – let everyone know who will be affected by the decision
- **check** – monitor effectiveness and review.

Using diagrams and graphs can help to clarify a particular situation and aid decision-making. For example, a cause and effect diagram can be helpful in concentrating minds on exactly what issues need to be taken into account when coming to a decision. You start with the problem on the far right and then lead back adding all possible causes until there are lots of ideas which spring from, or lead to, yet others. This will then give you starting points for problem solving.

For instance, if you were seeking to improve the telephone answering in the surgery during the early morning busy period, you might consider the following possible causes of the problem:

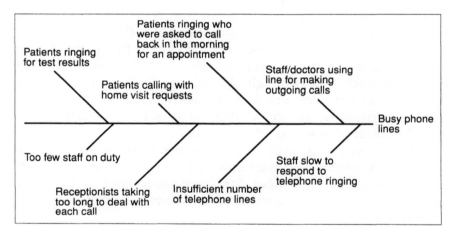

Figure 1: Possible causes of busy phone lines in the early morning.

In order to discover as many causes as possible, brainstorming can be a useful way of filling in the grid. Brainstorming, if you have not come across it before, is a very useful way of eliciting as many ideas as possible by the simple expedient of getting everyone to suggest any thought associated with the main topic that comes into their heads, however improbable it might seem. A sound idea can often be derived from even the most obscure or seemingly ridiculous ideas, and it is important that all contributions are written down and given equal value if the system is to work well. Eventually a full picture will emerge made up of the ideas produced during such a brainstorming session. One of the strengths of this system is that one person's idea can lead to several suggestions on the same theme from others, which in turn can lead to yet more.

One of the most important things to remember in decision-making in general practice is to take accurate minutes of any agreements reached at meetings where important issues are discussed. Minutes should be indexed in such a way that previous discussions and agreements on the same subject can be brought before the meeting. A card index is all that is required if you do not normally keep a record of the minutes on a word-processor, in which case a search facility for key words would probably suffice. On the card should be written the subject heading and the date of any meetings at which the subject was discussed. It is then an easy matter to refer back through the minute book to the date in question and note any previous decisions made on the subject. This is particularly helpful if there is disagreement among the partners about what was actually agreed.

Nothing you can do will ensure that the partners agree all the time but by taking a rational approach to decision-making, you can at least hope to achieve firm agreements and a degree of compliance in carrying out the necessary actions to make the plans come to fruition.

▲ Question 35: Control

I have recently been appointed practice manager in a large practice with more than 20 staff. Previously I worked in a small practice where we were few in number and were able to cover most of the different jobs between us. What differences might I have to make to my style of management to suit this larger practice?

It is difficult to make the initial adjustments required to work in a new practice with its inherent organizational structure that almost certainly differs substantially from that in your previous practice (if only because of their relative sizes). The main difference in the management style required will almost certainly be in those issues relating to the scale of the job. Because the practice is much larger there will naturally be more to manage – more people, more services, larger premises, more complex finances, more going on in general. On the other hand, you will also have a greater number of staff to whom you can delegate (*see* Question **30**). Although you will have far more responsibility in a large practice, there will always be other members of staff who can take on many of the more mundane tasks associated with various aspects of the practice. You may have to offer individuals additional training to enable them to take on this extra responsibility, but once they are established you will be more free to concentrate on the wider view.

You will find that in order to manage the larger practice effectively, you will have to give more of your time and attention to planning and organizing, and correspondingly less to directing and controlling. Directing is about implementing and carrying out plans through subordinates to achieve specific objectives. Controlling includes setting objectives, evaluating and amending according to end results and can mean working through an audit cycle. Both directing and controlling will naturally have to remain part of your management role, but the proportion of time you spend on them will have to be reduced if you are to make time for planning.

If you delegate more of the day-to-day control, you will be able to stand back in order to gain an overview of the practice and possible ways forward. It is all too easy to become bogged down in the detail of managing the daily activities of the practice and forget to raise your eyes to the horizon. The GPs will often have little time or inclination to do this themselves so it is important that you, as manager, make the time to step back and take a wider perspective of the whole business. This is true management. You can then be more proactive, planning more effectively for the future and resisting the temptation to continue merely reacting to changes imposed externally.

▲ Question 36: Managing appearances – first impressions

Our practice is in health authority premises and is somewhat shabby and usually rather untidy. Are there any inexpensive ways of improving the first impression the surgery makes on patients?

One effective and relatively inexpensive way of smartening up the appearance of your practice and influencing the first impression that it makes on visitors, is for the reception staff to wear uniforms. Not only does this look good but it is also practical and enables members of the reception staff to be easily identified. In practices where the staff do not wear a uniform, women GPs will tell you that when they stray into reception, patients often assume them to be a receptionist – such is the public's perception of the likely role of women in general practice. This can also happen in reverse to male managers who are invariably taken for a doctor.

Uniforms not only enable staff to be easily recognized, they also prevent staff from wearing inappropriate clothes such as jeans. The cost to the practice of supplying a simple uniform for each member of staff need not be great. The days when staff wore white coats, like hospital doctors or vets, has passed. However, if you can agree a basic colour with the staff (and it certainly pays to involve all staff in the discussions right from the start), then the choice of actual style of outfit could be left to the individual. For example, if you decide to have navy skirts and cardigans with a plain white blouse, most clothes shops would be likely to stock something suitable in an appropriate style.

If you feel a more co-ordinated look would better suit your particular practice, you might choose a special range from a mail-order catalogue. But do check that the particular style you have selected is not likely to be discontinued in the foreseeable future and make sure, before you decide, that the clothes are stocked in all the sizes your staff are likely to require.

The GPs should specify how much they are prepared to pay staff in the first year to cover the initial outlay, and how much in subsequent years for replacement items. Many of the staff will already be able to find some articles of clothing in their wardrobes which might fit into the scheme – but everyone should be given the same budget.

In my experience staff are usually happy not to have the problem of deciding what to wear to work any more. As long as the clothes are comfortable and practical, and not too restrictive, a uniform gives them a sense of corporate identity, a feeling of belonging and enables them to feel part of the team.

Another way of improving first impressions is to require all staff to wear name badges. It has become common policy for staff working in hospitals to wear a name badge so that they can easily be identified – why not in general practice also? I am particularly keen that staff have their full name, not just their first name on their badges but some staff who live within the practice area might prefer not to have their surname known for personal reasons and this preference should be respected. Another alternative might be to have their job title only on the badge.

What about the appearance of the premises? If the doctors do not own the surgery, there is little you can do except beg the health authority, or whoever owns the building, to redecorate. All practices, however, can have fresh plants and flowers and current issues of magazines which will help to make the waiting areas more attractive. Some surgeries have a tropical fish tank on display but be sure to have a volunteer among the staff who is willing to take responsibility for the fish if this is what you decide. The tank will also have to be placed out of reach of children for safety reasons.

You might decide to have piped music in the waiting areas. This can help prevent people from overhearing private conversations at the reception desk or in consulting rooms. However, it can also irritate if the wrong kind of music is being played. You should also investigate any possible requirements for the practice to hold a broadcasting licence or to pay royalties to artists whose music you play.

Notice boards displaying patient information should be kept neat and any out-of-date posters discarded. Information leaflets should be regularly updated and kept on a rack in reach of adults but not children.

First appearances are important – the practice should be welcoming not only to patients but also to doctors, staff and occasional visitors. Working in pleasant surroundings can make a difference to the efficiency with which people undertake their jobs and this in turn leads to benefits for patients.

▲ Question 37: Quality management

What is TQM and how is it relevant to general practice?

TQM stands for Total Quality Management. It is not simply a management buzzword but a system of ensuring that everyone in an organization is aware that their performance affects the end consumer of the service or product. Firms practising TQM motivate staff to ensure that the service they offer is provided to a consistent standard. This means establishing a culture where certain standards are agreed for how things should be done, and which then strives to attain them and even improve on them. Everyone in the practice will need to work within an agreed framework to provide a satisfactory level of service for patients but to do this well the doctors and staff will first have to learn how to work effectively in a team.

Irvine and Irvine assert that 'Quality is an absolute... like beauty, justice and truth' and state that it is far more difficult to assess the quality of healthcare than it is to decide whether a particular product is of good quality or not.[9] One definition of quality in the health service is when a patient receives the treatment from all the quarters that they hoped for and expected. This seems to be a rather tall order and patients will of course differ in their expectations of what actually constitutes adequate treatment.

Some will simply require a clear diagnosis from their GP, while others will seek a shoulder to cry on and good bedside manner. Some patients will feel that a warm and welcoming practice is the ideal, while others will be more concerned with access for push-chairs or wheelchairs.

Brooks and Borgardts identify two main requirements for achieving TQM.[10] These are:

- absolute commitment and leadership from the partners
- a positive organizational culture which involves having an agreed philosophy for the practice, based on shared values that are understood by all the staff.

Agreeing and setting standards and targets is an essential part of TQM and working towards achieving an agreed level of performance, attainable in a given period, should be the next step. Monitoring performance and producing a business plan should be incorporated into the quality control system and to monitor processes in general practice it will be necessary to undertake regular audit (*see* Question **39**).

▲ Question 38: Quality circles

Can you explain what a quality circle is and exactly how I might use the concept in the practice?

Quality circles originated in Japan and involve small groups of workers meeting together to identify, discuss and find solutions to problems they are experiencing in their work. The people most likely to find solutions to a problem are the individuals who are encountering the problem daily. There are many advantages in having quality circles, not least of which is the additional interest and job satisfaction that it offers to the staff. It provides an opportunity for personal development, improving their problem-solving abilities and serves to improve relationships within the group and with the manager and GPs.

The advantages from the business point of view are that more effective teamwork and increased productivity should result. There is also likely to be less absenteeism or staff turnover if employees feel they are an essential part of the organization and that they have some control over their working environment. An example of how to use a quality circle might be in finding ways of solving the problem of misfiled medical records – the senior receptionist, the filing clerk (if you have one) and perhaps one or two of the other receptionists who spend time filing can all sit down together and search for ways of improving the system. They might discuss some of the following ideas:

- the use of tracers
- colour-coding the notes
- re-labelling notes where the name is difficult to decipher
- altering the shelving in some way to improve accessibility of records
- preventing GPs from removing records (and losing them in their cars).

The group can then inform the manager of their suggestions and those ideas considered to be the most effective can be tried out. It would then be necessary to review the situation after an agreed period, to see if the new systems are working as planned.

Participating in quality circles helps staff to feel they are actively involved in improving their particular area of work and, ultimately have some say in the development of the practice. Gradually, as individuals learn to ask questions and find the answers themselves from discussion with their peers, they will come to see innovation as an important part of working life. They will see that the introduction of change can bring advantages and perhaps therefore be more sympathetic to changes suggested by others.

▲ Question 39: Audit

The practice has been involved in clinical audit for several years but I want to try auditing administrative procedures as well. Where should I start?

There are many systems within most practices that can usefully be audited, e.g. telephone usage, telephone answering, availability of appointments, repeat prescription procedures and contraceptive claims. These can all be monitored and audited to determine whether the current system is working to best effect or whether there are ways in which it might be improved. Irvine and Irvine state that audit can 'help simplify the organization of work and so take some of the stress out of life. It can show whether or not a practice is achieving what it set out to do.'[11]

It is likely that you are undertaking a kind of informal audit most of the time as you scrutinize some of the systems you have in the practice and continually seek to improve their effectiveness. If this is undertaken in a more formal manner, working through the whole audit cycle, the process can be more scientific and precise (*see* Figure 2).

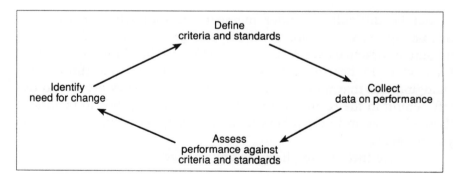

Figure 2: The audit circle.[11]

You will need to define your criteria and set standards, collect data on current performance, assess this performance against your original criteria and standards and then identify any need for change. Once you have done this, you can amend your procedure and then repeat the process to see if you have achieved the result you wanted.

The Medical Audit Advisory Group (MAAG) or Clinical Outcomes Audit Group (COAG) are particularly helpful in advising practices in the selection of suitable areas for audit and the ways in which you can set realistic standards and establish appropriate criteria. Once you have undertaken your first audit, you will begin to appreciate the value of the process to the management of the practice as a whole. You will find that you are assessing the effectiveness of all your procedures on a regular basis and this can only lead to greater efficiency.

▲ Question 40: Managing change

We have two receptionists who have been with us for many years. They find it difficult to accept change and, in particular, find accessing data on the computer difficult. How can I help them accept that they have to move with the times?

It can be difficult for older members of staff who are used to manual systems, to adapt to all the changes that have taken place in general practice over recent years. It is also hard for some of the GPs who are nearing retirement age to accept that things are changing and that they will need to adapt too, if they are not to be left behind in the relentless march forward. Your job is to facilitate these changes and help others to adjust, carrying them with you as you progress.

There are three main phases to any change:

1 the current state

2 the transition state
3 the planned future state.

It might help to prepare a force field diagram to show at a glance the main resisting and driving forces which are likely to be involved in the transition state as you move towards achieving the desired change. In the situation where long-serving staff are resistant to change the diagram might look like the one in Figure 3.

The thickness of the arrows denotes the strength of the particular force. If you draw up a diagram like this for your particular situation, you should then be able to determine the various courses of action you will need to take in order to advance.

In the example given, a need for training in the use of the computer has been identified. You might want to undertake this on a one-to-one basis for the staff concerned as this would be seen as far less threatening than having to learn in a group – remember that IT training is a skill in itself. You will need to offer encouragement and support to the individuals concerned so that they gradually lose their fears and gain confidence in their new skills.

If the particular members of staff choose not to adapt and accept

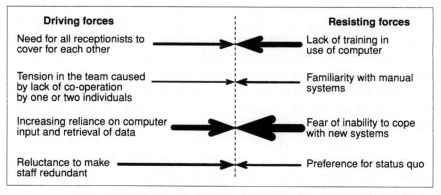

Figure 3: Force field diagram showing relevant strength of forces for and against staff adapting to change.

training, you are faced with two alternatives. If they are close to retirement, you might decide to allocate them different duties which will not require use of the computer, e.g. filing or pulling notes for surgeries. On the other hand, if they are unwilling to accept such a role you will be forced to offer them redundancy as there will no longer be a role for any receptionists who are not computer-literate.

▲ Question 41: SWOT analysis

I have heard people speak of the value of undertaking a SWOT analysis in general practice. Just what does this mean and how do I go about it?

SWOT is an acronym that stands for the **strengths**, **weaknesses**, **opportunities** and **threats** of an organization. It is unfortunate that a SWOT analysis is often viewed with suspicion by GPs who see it as just another futile management process with little relevance to general practice. It can, in fact, be a very useful way of identifying possible future developments that will impinge on or be required in the practice. Examples might include the setting up of a new health centre within the practice catchment area (an obvious threat); the building of a large housing development nearby (a possible opportunity to increase the patient list); two partners of near-retirement age who might decide to retire within months of each other in the next two years (weakness); a loyal and dedicated staff (strength). All these are events that will undoubtedly affect decision-making when deliberating about the future of the practice.

In order to identify aspects of the practice which might have a bearing on the analysis, it is often helpful to have a brainstorming session where everyone present makes suggestions that are noted and expanded on later. Brainstorming is defined by Chambers *et al.* as a widely used technique for generating ideas that depends for its effectiveness on 'keeping options open and suspending judgement.'[12] They go on to say that those participating will offer ideas more willingly if others agree not to rush to evaluate them immediately. This is particularly true at a general meeting in which those present might be working in a relatively junior capacity in the practice and would be unwilling to put forward ideas if others more senior were likely to offer criticism. Brainstorming sessions are known for often producing seemingly wild suggestions which, on reflection and with amendment, can produce useful ideas for consideration.

A SWOT analysis can be undertaken at an away day (*see* Question **24**) and can be a helpful preliminary, for example, to writing a feasibility study for a specific project or even a first step towards producing a full business plan (*see* Question **42**).

▲ Question 42: Business plan

I understand that some practices have produced a business plan. Is this essential and, if so, what do I need to include?

It is not only fundholding practices that require business plans. Any practice that wants to retain some semblance of control over its development should be prepared to spend time producing such a plan. Some of the points which should be included in a business plan are:[13]

- the specific aims and objectives of the practice
- a SWOT analysis
- the management structure of the practice
- members of the team, their particular roles and lines of authority
- list of services that are currently provided, together with proposals for future services
- cash flow projection and forecast of profits

- outside commitments of partners
- the partners' roles within the practice and how these might be developed.

Other questions have dealt with producing a SWOT analysis (*see* Question **41**) and identifying your current management structure (*see* Question **14**). Cash flow will be dealt with more fully in the next book in this series. In brief, however, cash flow projections are an invaluable tool for good financial management. By listing anticipated income and expenditure month-by-month for the following year against the various sources of income and expenditure headings, an estimated balance can be carried forward each month enabling profit levels to be estimated.

Once you have looked at all the above points in relation to the practice, you should be able to write a simple business plan which will enable the team to work towards the desired objectives.

The purpose of the business plan should be to provide a blueprint of where the practice is now, where it wants to be in the future and what steps will be required to achieve those ends. Each practice will want to emphasize different aspects of their strategy in their plan. All the partners and staff should be involved in the discussions so that there is no danger of them feeling that the finished plan has been imposed on them. If everyone feels involved in the deliberations, then production of the plan can be a unifying experience for the whole team. You are also more likely to receive the support and co-operation of the staff in achieving the objectives if they have been involved in the plan's preparation.

▲ Question 43: Player/manager

Our practice has a list size of only 3000 patients and a husband and wife team of GPs is in partnership. I have to combine the role of practice manager and medical secretary. I also help out in reception when required and at the moment seldom have time for anything other than dealing with crises as they occur. Can you give me any tips on how to make time for actual management?

I am not sure which is the more difficult: to be a practice manager who was once a receptionist but is now required purely to manage the practice, or be expected to do a little of everything. The former (which is dealt with in Question 44) means that you have to persuade both GPs and staff that you are no longer available to help out in your old role because you need to concentrate all your energies on management. In smaller practices you have the equally unenviable task of trying to wear several hats at the same time, a not unusual situation. A small practice normally cannot afford to employ a full-time practice manager and may compromise by asking one member of staff to cover several roles.

The easiest way to ensure that you have dedicated management time is to designate certain times of the day, or days of the week for strategic planning. At such times you need to make it known that you are not available to help out in reception or deal with secretarial tasks. Unfortunately, by its very nature general practice is full of crises of varying magnitude and you will inevitably be called upon to cope with an emergency in one department or another when you are not, strictly speaking, available. However, by allocating certain times solely for management activity, you should be able to shut the office door and concentrate on planning, forecasting and all the other myriad tasks which are required of an effective manager.

▲ Question 44: Poacher turned gamekeeper

I have recently been appointed practice manager. I previously worked as a receptionist for seven years in the same practice and am now finding it difficult to make the transition. Are there any simple ways in which I can distance myself from the day-to-day workings of reception?

It is often hard to drop the old role completely and adjust to the new one – transition is never easy. Adams, Hayes and Hopson identify phases that you can expect to go through in any transition and include experiencing disruption, gradually acknowledging its reality, testing oneself, understanding oneself and then incorporating change in one's behaviour.[14]

In the beginning there will probably be a temptation to spend all your time operating rather than managing. You might believe that it helps your leadership image if you show that you can still do anything that you ask members of staff to do. It often seems quicker and easier to do the job yourself rather than leave it to somebody who perhaps will not do it as well as you. This is denying the reality of your new role. If you are going to become a true manager, you will have to learn to delegate (*see* Question 30). You cannot forever be available to 'help out in reception' and at the same time manage other aspects of the practice which demand your attention.

You might take the opportunity to develop the staff, offering them opportunities to improve their skills and gain valuable experience. Is it fair that you continue to do tasks which others are capable of doing and learning from? After all, who knows better than a former receptionist the frustrations of working in reception? You should perhaps emphasize the democratic form of leadership, consulting colleagues rather than imposing your decisions on them. If you can carry them with you by showing that you have their interests at heart, as well as those of the partners and the practice, then they will probably offer you their whole-hearted support.

3

Communicating

Good communication is vital in any business and without it there can be no progress or development, staff will be unhappy and the employer will become increasingly alienated from the workforce.

Communication is about conveying ideas and feelings. It is no good telling people something if they are not able to understand what you are saying or worse still, are not listening to you. Research has shown that managers spend a large proportion of their time, sometimes as much as 80%, giving and receiving information. This might be in written form such as reports, memos, letters, agendas, minutes or notes. Included in this section are several questions on various aspects of written communication; report-writing and note-taking, both of which are essential to the management of any business. You will need to know how to write succinct letters which are clear and unambiguous. You will also need to record the deliberations and agreements at practice meetings – minute-taking is a special skill, requiring accuracy and brevity.

It is possible to communicate less formally by the spoken word. Indeed, non-verbal communication such as body language, eye contact or tone of voice are an integral part of this form of communication and can have a dramatic impact on the message being conveyed. For the listener, as well as the speaker, posture is important. How you sit can convey your attitude towards the speaker and what they have to say. Listening to someone whilst sitting in a 'closed' position with legs and arms crossed can be very off-putting and denotes a level of defensiveness on your part and a reluctance to accept what the speaker has to say. On the other hand, if you lean forward, make good eye contact, nod occasionally and reflect back some of the points the speaker is making, you reassure them that you are listening with an open mind and are absorbing what they are saying.

The questions in this section cover most areas of communication. Many are particularly relevant to general practice with special emphasis on the importance of running effective meetings, respecting confidentiality, the need for patient feedback and the importance of networking. If you can master the art of communicating effectively, you will have the necessary foundation for providing sound management.

▲ Question 45: Meetings

Our GPs always complain when I suggest that a meeting is necessary to discuss some important project. They get even more cross when I suggest that a follow-up meeting might be required. Is there a way of convincing them of the relevance of such meetings.

Most GPs seem to dislike and distrust meetings and seldom acknowledge the need for regular meetings, let alone a requirement for a formal agenda and minutes. Huntingdon proposes that 'GPs would tolerate meetings more readily if they were perceived to be productive, if needed decisions were made and subsequently implemented.'[15]

You therefore have to prove to them that by meeting they are achieving something which they will find worthwhile, if not immediately, then in the near future. The way to achieve this is to manage the meetings so well that they are not only kept brief and purposeful but are also profitable as far as aiding decision-making or information-sharing are concerned.

I read somewhere that meetings should be 'a communication device, a cauldron of creativity in which new ideas are born, and an anvil on which solid plans are forged'. I can think of many meetings that have not approached that ideal by any stretch of the imagination but it is an admirable goal to aim for. Meetings satisfy a deep instinct in all of us to communicate with others, to share common problems, opinions and attitudes. Before deciding on a formal meeting, however, it is essential to make sure that the meeting is really necessary. Would a memo do instead? A conference call? Individual executive action followed by circulation of details?

Some of the most likely reasons for holding a meeting are:[16]

- to legitimize and empower
- to create a springboard for action
- to increase the knowledge base
- to pool ideas and exchange information
- to serve the process of democratic management
- to build morale
- to make policy
- to facilitate structured planning.

Most practice meetings involve several of the above, depending on the subject and actual participants. With so many people now working in general practice – attached staff, fundholding team, complementary therapists, retained doctors – it is important that all are kept informed and are permitted to participate in aspects of the practice which directly affect them. Clinical meetings to include nurses and GPs, and staff meetings for ancillary staff will be required at monthly or quarterly intervals. Budget meetings for the fundholding team and representatives of the local trust or HA will also be required on a regular, if not necessarily frequent, basis.

Meetings can fail for many reasons and it is important to ensure that this does not happen to you. Ask yourself the following questions:

- is the meeting really necessary?
- is the agenda concise?
- have relevant papers been circulated in advance?
- is the meeting being held at the right time and place?
- is the time allowed too long, or too short?
- is the chairperson effective? (*see* Question **49**)
- will accurate minutes be taken?
- who will see that action points are carried out?

If the meeting is well planned, adequately chaired and an accurate record is kept of the proceedings, those present should feel a sense of achievement when they leave the meeting rather than a feeling of disillusion and waste of time. If this is how meetings in your practice are run, the GPs will be more inclined to attend.

▲ Question 46: Staff meetings

I find it difficult to persuade staff to attend meetings regularly. If they do come, they seldom participate in the meeting but are always keen to voice criticism of the proceedings afterwards. How can I encourage greater involvement and commitment?

Finding the right time to hold a staff meeting is never easy. By their very nature surgeries are open long hours and staff often have to be available until 7 p.m. or even later in the evenings. An evening meeting is therefore seldom likely to be a success.

Perhaps the best time to have a staff meeting is during the lunch hour. If you normally keep your surgery open during the lunch-break, you could ask one of the GPs if they are willing to cover the phones/desk for an hour while the rest of the staff meet. Alternatively you could make the decision to close the surgery 'for staff training' and put a notice on the door well in advance to warn patients.

It is difficult to persuade part-time staff to attend on a day when they would normally not be working. You will just have to choose a day when the least number of part-timers are likely to be absent and then try to persuade everyone to attend. You can offer over-time pay as an inducement, or time in lieu might be a cheaper and preferable option. Providing a simple sandwich lunch is also an added incentive to encourage attendance.

Let us assume that you have managed to persuade everyone to turn up. Now you have the problem of getting them to participate. If you have circulated or posted up an agenda in advance (which will include items that they wish to discuss as well as ones you have submitted), they will have had time to marshal their thoughts and decide what they want to say. You will need to chair the meeting with care, encouraging everyone to have their say, uninterrupted by others. You must show that you are taking note of what they are saying, perhaps by summarizing their contributions occasionally and minuting salient points.

At the end of the meeting it is important to state and note in the minutes what the agreements have been and what the action points are. These should be circulated or put on a notice-board for everyone to see as soon after the meeting as possible. It is then up to you to see that people do in fact carry out the things that they have been asked to do before the next meeting.

In my experience most people are happy to attend a meeting if they can see the point of it and a positive outcome results, with direct action being taken. If you learn how to hold successful meetings, you should be guaranteed a good attendance.

▲ Question 47: Setting agendas

I am expected to set the agenda for the weekly practice meeting. I am occasionally at a loss, since the doctors seldom give me any idea of what they would like to discuss in advance, and choose instead to bring matters up under 'any other business'. What can I do?

It is an impossible situation if matters are raised on the day with no one receiving advance notification of what is to be discussed. The agenda needs to include all the main subjects for discussion and these should not number more than three or four at the most. You will not have time to devote to more than a few main issues and if the agenda is too long there is a danger that only hurried superficial discussion will take place and no real agreements will be reached. Only relatively trivial last-minute items should be raised under 'any other business'.

You should impress upon the partners the desirability of knowing in advance what will be coming up for discussion. They can then prepare by doing relevant research or, more probably, asking you to look up the necessary information. For the majority of practice business meetings you will find that most of the matters for discussion will be the ones that you wish to raise. Because GPs are usually so busy, it can be very difficult to catch them during the working day to discuss the management of the business and so regular practice meetings are essential to provide a forum for discussion of important issues. You can only hope that it soon becomes apparent to the doctors that matters which are on the agenda are more likely to be discussed in full than those which are introduced without prior warning under AOB. They will eventually begin to realise the value of informing you in advance of items they would like added to the agenda.

▲ Question 48: Taking minutes

Who should take the minutes at our practice meetings? Does it always have to be me? And just what should I record?

It doesn't have to be you if you feel this is inappropriate. If the subjects under discussion are not confidential, it would be in order to have a secretary take the minutes and you could then approve the draft before it was circulated. However, in my experience, it is often more efficient and convenient for the practice manager to minute any agreements reached at practice meetings, even if you are also trying to chair the meeting at the same time. There is no reason why, at the end of each agenda item, you should not just briefly summarize the discussion and agreed course of action and note it down as a minute. You can always expand it from memory later if necessary. It is often quite helpful for all those present to have a brief recap of the discussion so that everyone can be sure they have understood just what it is they have agreed to.

Minutes should be kept as brief as possible. No one, least of all any of the busy doctors, is going to want to wade through verbatim notes of what was discussed. For a subject that is likely to prove particularly contentious in the future, or occasions where there is a wide range of opinions among the partners, then it might be wise to take more detailed notes for future reference. You will soon learn just what you need to record, if only because when you look back and refer to previous minutes you will realise just what is missing, what should have been included and what seems surplus to requirements.

▲ Question 49: Chairing a meeting

Our senior partner always insists on chairing practice meetings but he is hopeless. Mostly he just holds forth himself, often not addressing the agenda item under discussion. The other partners are unable to put their point of view and if they do get a word in he often disregards their opinion. What can I do to improve things?

It is not uncommon in general practice for the longest serving partner to feel that it is incumbent on them to chair all meetings. One suggestion might be to ask some of the other partners if they would be prepared to act as chairman, perhaps in rotation, and then with their backing put the suggestion to the senior partner. You could point out that the other doctors need the experience if they are to learn how to chair a meeting effectively. You could also stress that it might permit him to participate more fully in the general discussion, if he is not at the same time having to control the meeting.

The mnemonic WHIP is my way of remembering the ideal attributes of a chairman of a meeting: **W** is for wisdom, **H** is for the hide of a rhinoceros, **I** is for impartiality, **P** is for patience. If you possess these characteristics then perhaps you might be the most appropriate person to chair the partners' meeting.

A good chairman should enable everyone present to contribute to the meeting. Meetings should be productive or they will be seen as a complete waste of time. It is therefore particularly important that you make the necessary changes as soon as possible to ensure that the senior partner learns to take a back seat occasionally, and that everyone can participate fully.

▲ Question 50: Isolation

Before taking the job of practice manager I hadn't realised just how much I would be working in isolation. The doctors seldom seem to have time to spend with me or show any interest in discussing management matters – there is no one else on the staff with whom it seems appropriate to do this. Can you suggest how I might reduce this feeling of working in a vacuum?

Many practice managers feel as you do. You are not alone although it may seem that way! You need to persuade the GPs to meet with you, perhaps individually and certainly as a partnership, to discuss matters relating to the management of the practice.

If the GPs do not already have individual responsibility for certain areas of management within the practice, such as the finances, personnel or computers, then you might suggest they allocate these among themselves, perhaps on a rotating basis. You should plan to have a regular informal meeting with the designated partner at a set time each week. In my experience such meetings often had to be postponed, deferred or cancelled because of emergencies or holidays but at least you can be sure of some regular contact if you write it into the calendar. Partners' meetings to discuss business matters should also be held at least once a month, and perhaps more frequently in a large practice. It is essential that you have an opportunity to speak to them all together and just as important that they have the chance to speak to each other on matters affecting the organization of their practice.

If the meetings are kept as short as possible and are always relevant and helpful, then you should have no problem in obtaining general agreement to your plans (*see* Question **45**).

You are right in thinking that there is seldom any member of staff with whom you can discuss business matters relating to the practice, or indeed the staff. If your neutrality is to remain evident you have to be seen to 'walk by yourself'. If you are to keep in touch with the latest developments and new ideas perhaps you could liaise with colleagues in other practices who are doing a similar job (*see* Question **51**).

▲ Question 51: Networking

I find it difficult to come up with innovative ideas for running the practice. My contact with the partners is minimal due to work pressures on them and I would welcome ideas of where I can get both support and new ideas.

One of the best ways of compensating for the solitary nature of your work is to network with colleagues in other practices. You can do this on an informal basis via telephone to the manager of another local practice, or you could investigate the possibility of joining a local practice managers' group – the HA should be able to give you the contact for one in your area. If you belong to the Association of Managers in General Practice (AMGP) you could ask them for details of any local branch. Local branch meetings often include a speaker who takes a topical theme for their talk that is particularly relevant to practice managers.

You might also consider occasionally attending a conference for practice managers such as the General Practice '97 conference run in May each year at the NEC in Birmingham (contact Sterling Events whose address is given in *Useful addresses* on p. 111). The AMGP hold an annual conference as does the Institute of Health Services Management (IHSM) and you will usually find details of these advertised in *Practice Manager*. Most practices also receive the information directly, although it may be addressed to the senior partner – so keep an eye on his in-tray.

Attendance at any of these conferences will enable you to network with colleagues working in other practices in different parts of the country and provide you with the opportunity to compare notes. It is also comforting to realise that many of the problems you experience with the partners and the practice are duplicated in others. You can even occasionally discuss confidential practice matters without fear of your particular doctors being identified, once you have established that their practice is in the Outer Hebrides or Penzance and many miles from your own. At one such conference, I remember being told some hair-raising tales about one particular practice where the manager was aware that the GPs were extensively defrauding the NHS but felt powerless to prevent it. It was good for him to share his concern, knowing that everything he said would be treated in confidence. I was able to identify various courses of action which he could consider taking, the first of which was to confront the partners and tell them of his disquiet.

If it is ideas, rather than personal contact, that you are missing, then you can spend some time each week reading the GP newspapers (*Pulse*, *GP* and *Doctor*) and various journals (*Practice Manager*, *Medeconomics*, *Financial Pulse* and the *BMA News*

Review) to gather new ideas that have worked in other practices. Why re-invent the wheel when you can adapt the innovative ideas of others? These journals are a useful source of information on what is happening in the NHS and details of any proposed changes the government intends to introduce into primary care will be charted, and possible implications for GPs will be explored.

It is important that you keep in touch with what is going on in the wider world of the NHS and in other practices in the region. Do not become too isolated and introspective or you may get left behind in the constant changes that are occurring in primary care.

▲ Question 52: Negotiating

I hadn't realized that I would need to know how to negotiate when I became a practice manager. I thought just fund managers would need to negotiate contracts, but I find myself negotiating with the partners regarding staff pay and conditions and with the health authority on staff budgets. Can you give me some tips on how to negotiate successfully?

The most important piece of advice I was ever given on negotiating, from a skilled and experienced negotiator, was always to seek a 'win/win' situation in dealings with people where you want to achieve some particular objective.

Negotiating is usually easier if you are part of a team because you can then rehearse your arguments in advance. One of the team can play devil's advocate to enable the others to detect any weaknesses in their arguments prior to negotiations taking place. It is also helpful to have one person who takes a hard line, contrasted with another in the team who takes a softer line – this can be very effective in gaining concessions from the opposition. (This is usually known as the good cop/bad cop routine.)

However, if you have to negotiate alone with the GPs on staff matters, the first thing you should do is forearm yourself with all the information and figures you might require in order to put your case. Be prepared to concede some points and allow room in your initial 'demands' for such compromise. Remember that you want the other side to feel that they have also 'won' at the end of the discussion. If the other party feels aggrieved at the end of talks, feeling they have conceded too much, then the likelihood is that the outcome will not be a total success for anyone. Once you have reached agreement on the proposed way forward, make sure that you write down all the points discussed and obtain the signatures of those present if the subject is likely to prove contentious in the future.

To summarize, for successful negotiations you need to:

- do your research
- have facts and figures to hand
- be willing to concede some less essential points
- be prepared to compromise
- keep a written record of agreements reached.

▲ Question 53: Listening

I find I have to tell staff several times how I want things done. They don't seem to understand, or want to understand, what I am asking. How can I improve matters?

Listening effectively can really help to improve your impact as a manager. Not only will you hear what people are telling you, but there is a good chance that they will listen to what you have to say in return. There is a difference between hearing and listening; listening involves some participation in the process but in order to listen you need to stop talking yourself. Montgomery states that 'the key components in active listening are attending, interpreting and understanding'.[17]

You can show interest and prove you are attending by the use of body language such as nodding, or reflecting back what they have said. To do this appropriately, you have to choose the salient points in what the speaker has said and paraphrase them. You then repeat this and obtain their agreement to your interpretation of what they are saying. If your reflection is an accurate picture of what they have been trying to convey, the speaker realizes that you are comprehending what they are trying to tell you. To listen well, you also need to be patient and not be tempted to interrupt. Ask questions to encourage the speaker by all means but do not interrupt when they are speaking.

You may think that this does not answer the question posed but I can assure you that it does go some way towards doing so. It may be that you give orders without asking the staff for their view of the situation, or if you do ask them, perhaps you do not listen to their reply. If you learn to listen properly when someone is speaking to you, perhaps they will return the compliment.

▲ Question 54: Channels of communication

We have the builders in our surgery at the moment, and I have heard whispers that the staff have been complaining that they haven't been kept properly informed of what is happening. How can I improve the channels of communication?

When you are bound up in the complexities of managing a busy general practice, it is all too easy to overlook some aspect of communication. However, it is crucially important that everyone is kept informed as far as possible of matters that concern them and impinge on their working conditions. In particular, staff need to know about the likely progress in the building works and how it will affect their working conditions and access for the patients.

A notice-board in the main office with a programme of planned progress of the builders' schedule would be a useful start. A short informal staff meeting at the beginning of each week informing everyone of which particular parts of the building will be affected could also be helpful. The receptionists will be the ones who are most likely to be faced with the patients' complaints if access to the building is obstructed in any way. If the staff know in advance what is planned, they can make suitable preparations for putting up signs showing alternative entrances or apologizing for inconvenience to visitors.

Safety of staff and visitors alike is an issue too. All care should be taken to warn of potentially dangerous hazards such as scaffolding or rubble that might be obstructing pathways. The contractors will need to be extra vigilant in considering the safety of children and the elderly who are both regular visitors to any surgery.

It might be an idea for a member of staff to regularly patrol the area where the builders are working to ensure that everything possible is being done to reduce the disruption. There is seldom any way of reducing the noise levels that such work can create, but builders can sometimes be persuaded to do their noisiest drilling and sawing work during the middle of the day when there are likely to be fewer patients consulting. A good idea is to have a named member of staff from each group, i.e. one receptionist, one nurse, who can liaise with you. You can keep them posted of any last minute changes to the builders' schedule and the likely disruption that will be caused, and they can inform the rest of the team. In this way the information is cascaded down on a regular basis.

Building works in a busy environment such as a general practice can be a nightmare, however well planned and managed, but good information disseminated among all the staff can help to minimize potential disruption to the working of the practice.

▲ Question 55: Sharing information

I sometimes find it difficult to decide just which information that relates to the partnership I should share with staff, and which I should treat as confidential. The staff occasionally accuse me of not keeping them informed. I also find that one partner will confide in me personal things that he doesn't want to share with his partners. Can you advise me?

It is not always obvious just which information you should treat as confidential, and which you should share with staff. If you err on the side of caution and keep to yourself most of the business matters relating to the practice which are discussed with the GPs at practice meetings, the staff may feel marginalized and even alienated. Practice nurses in particular often feel, perhaps, justifiably, that they should know everything discussed in practice meetings. Sometimes, however, it is not always appropriate for them to be present, e.g. if you are discussing delicate matters about disciplining a particular member of staff. You have to walk a fine line between, on the one hand, being unnecessarily secretive and not sharing information that is relevant and proper for staff to know, and on the other disclosing details about the partners or their finances which is inappropriate for anyone else to know about.

The point about individual partners confiding in you can be a problem in any practice. The doctors need to know that they can trust you to respect their confidence and not discuss personal matters, even with the other partners if this is what they ask. I found this role difficult when the matter under discussion was likely to have a large impact on the other partners, who really needed to be included in the discussions. I would try to encourage the doctor who was troubled at least to talk to one of his partners and seek support from him – however, if they refuse you have no option but to respect their wish and remain silent.

I can recall instances where a doctor was experiencing problems at home, and being concerned that he didn't feel able to share his worries with his partners at work. I have on occasion recommended that a GP seek help from one of the confidential advice lines that have been set up by fellow doctors for just such cases. There have been too many cases of suicide by a GP which perhaps resulted from a period of isolation and despair following a patient complaint.

▲ Question 56: Staff handbook

We recently appointed a new receptionist and found that our induction programme for her was very hit and miss. Have you any suggestions on how we can improve things for next time?

Your first step should be to appoint a mentor for any new member of staff, if you have not already done so. This applies to anyone, not just receptionists, and is a good way of ensuring that the new employee has a named member of staff to whom they can go when they have a question. There often seem to be so many questions in the first few days that it can be a great relief for a new recruit to know that there is a member of staff who has been specifically designated to answer their queries. It is helpful if the mentor can be relieved of some of their normal duties, at least for the first day or two to enable them to spend time with their charge. It is also only fair to choose a different mentor for the next new member of staff to be appointed. Sometimes the most recently appointed member of staff can help a newcomer best because they remember the sort of problems experienced.

A training programme should be drawn-up to enable the new staff member to acquire the necessary skills and knowledge. However, this should be spread over a period of time so that they are not expected to learn too much too quickly. There is training available specifically for medical receptionists such as the Radcliffe

PRP courses which are tailor-made for the particular needs of general practice reception staff.

Another element to any induction programme should be the production of a staff handbook. This ensures that new staff have at least some of the information they might require in their first weeks and months at work at their fingertips. In fact, the handbook should provide a handy reference point for all staff, not just the new ones and should contain the following:

- the names of all the doctors (including GP registrar, retained doctors and regular locums)
- the names and job titles of all the community staff attached to the practice
- a list of all the ancillary staff with whom they will come into contact
- addresses and telephone numbers of local hospitals and pathology lab
- information about uniforms and name badges
- a copy of the practice charter
- a sample contract of employment
- disciplinary and grievance procedure
- general housekeeping information, e.g. availability of showers, use of a microwave oven and coffee breaks
- details of health and safety procedures
- the location of the First Aid box and the accident book
- information regarding use of VDUs
- security matters
- information about private use of photocopier/fax/telephone.

A staff handbook is a simple but useful way of ensuring that information is readily available to any new or existing members of staff. New employees can read the handbook and feel that they know something of the ethos of the practice and what is expected of them as new recruits to the team.

▲ Question 57: Confidentiality

Our reception area behind the desk is open plan and most of the staff work at desks in clear view of the patients at reception. How can we talk to or about patients on the telephone without risking a breach of confidence?

Many practices have this problem. One of the most obvious ways of reducing the risk of people overhearing confidential conversations and identifying the subject, is not to use the name of the patient in your conversation. This goes against the instructions in most management manuals on customer service which stress the need to use the customer's name at periodic intervals during a telephone conversation. Receptionists should be made aware of the need to withhold names of callers at all times if there is any possibility of being overheard. Training of staff in respecting confidentiality at all times is essential together with increasing their awareness of the risks inherent in open plan reception areas.

At the desk it is often difficult to hold confidential conversations and so a small interview room just off the reception area is very useful if space permits. A member of staff can then talk to a patient in private without fear of being overheard. This room, as 'neutral' territory, can also be used to listen to any complaints by patients rather than the manager's own office.

There are obviously other issues relating to confidentiality within the practice which are not concerned with the patients but rather the business itself. For example, some GPs prefer that the finances of the practice are not discussed in front of junior staff, and quite understandably seek to keep private the details of their own income and the profitability of the practice. As practice manager you will almost certainly be privy to these matters and will be expected to treat them as confidential.

▲ Question 58: Liaison with other professionals

Because the GPs are often unavailable through pressure of work, it falls to me to liaise with the practice accountant and solicitor on financial and legal matters. What should I bear in mind when speaking to them?

The main thing to remember is that you are not a partner in the practice and as an employee it is your job to put the partners' point of view to outside agencies (there are a few non-medical partners in general practice, but they are very much the exception to the rule). In order to discover the partners' point of view it is usually necessary to hold a meeting at which general agreement is reached. When there are five or six GPs in a partnership, however, it is often difficult to obtain consensus on anything. If there is a strong difference of opinion on any particular point, e.g. on one of the clauses to be included in the partnership agreement, I would insist that all the partners discuss it at a meeting with the solicitor. A legally binding agreement is too important a document to include statements that do not reflect the views of all the existing partners.

Liaising with the accountant can be an expensive business. If no prior agreement is reached, the annual fee charged is likely to be based on the amount of work done during the year by the accountant or his staff. This can mean that every telephone call is logged and charged for. It is preferable to negotiate an all-inclusive fee which allows for occasional calls at no extra charge and it is in the accountant's interest to receive financial information in the format which it is simplest for him to process. It is therefore vital that you obtain from him details of how he would like the accounts submitted, e.g. can you transfer the cashbook and quarterly statement spreadsheets on disk in a format compatible with the accountant's system? If the work the accountant does is minimized because you have completed all the preliminary analysis, then the fee should be reduced accordingly and you can be sure that your hourly rate of pay will be considerably less than the accountant's.

There are of course other professionals with whom you might come into contact while representing the practice. For example, you might be required to liaise with an architect designing new premises or extending the present surgery; you will certainly need to co-operate with the managers of the local NHS trusts and your health authority; you might need to keep in contact with the community health council and other such agencies. At all times you will be representing the partners and so it is important that you get it right and create a good impression.

▲ Question 59: Making useful notes

Can you suggest some quick and effective ways of making notes as a preliminary to writing a report?

There are several ways of jotting down ideas which may prove useful as a prompt when writing a report – it rather depends on just what kind of report you have in mind. The annual report requires you to gather together a large number of statistics but the health authority may issue you with a pro forma for completion. You will therefore probably not need to plan the report to any large extent unless you intend adding free text to give the practice a record of events during the year.

However, if you want to make sure that you cover all the relevant issues, Tony Buzan's technique for 'mind mapping' is one of the most effective ways. This is a useful technique which takes advantage of the fact that many of us function rather better with images than with lines of text. He suggests that 'rather than starting from the top and working down in sentences or lists, one should start from the centre or main idea and branch out as dictated by the individual ideas and general form of the central theme.'[18] Begin with your main subject and write down any ideas that come to mind on a line leading from (or to) the centre. Other ideas can be added in turn joined to newly created branches of the map. For example, the practice might be opening a branch surgery and you need to consider all the relevant facts, cost implications, staffing requirements and any other possible ramifications (*see* Figure 4).

Once you have completed your pattern, the required information should be readily available for you to compose your report and all you now need to do is decide on the order of presenting the information. You can circle and number the individual ideas so that you end-up with a template for your proposed report which should reduce the time required to draft and re-draft the final paper. However messy your pattern may appear, it will be sufficient if it includes the relevant information and demonstrates the links between different points.

I have already mentioned brainstorming in answer to another question, but it also has relevance as a way of forming notes in

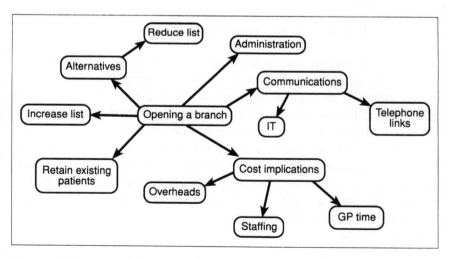

Figure 4: Mind map of ideas for feasibility report on opening a branch surgery.

preparation for a project. For example, if you are looking at the possibility of making acupuncture available at the surgery, you might want to seek suggestions from members of staff as to the feasibility of this before writing a report. They might mention some of the following:

- the availability of a suitable room on a regular basis
- the likely uptake by patients of the service
- the chance of all the GPs agreeing to the suggestion
- how will the practitioner be paid
- what safeguards against stray needles can be put in place
- will the cleaner need special instructions on how to deal with the hazard of used needles.

The ideas gathered from a group of people can be jotted down randomly as and when suggested from which patterns then emerge and links established between different individual ideas. Again an image is created which enables you to pick out those points that are relevant and important and those that are not. On their own one person cannot think of every possible point for consideration. Brainstorming offers an opportunity for everyone to contribute ideas and thus reduce the possibility of overlooking something important.

When note-taking during a discussion, it is important to ensure that you jot down only the key words or concepts. The words you choose have to trigger a memory if they are to prove reliable indicators of just what was discussed. A verbatim report of all the subjects covered will not necessarily be very helpful, not least because you will have been so busy making notes that you will not have paid sufficient attention to the content and emphasis of what was being said. So try to identify the major points as you go along. You can always interrupt the discussion at an appropriate moment to check that the points you have noted are the ones that were indeed stressed.

▲ Question 60: Writing a reference

One of our reception staff has recently left the practice and approached me to ask whether I would be willing to write a reference for her. She is currently applying for medical receptionist jobs in the area to which she and her husband have moved. My problem is that we were quite glad when she left. Her work was fine but she was unable to work well in a team and caused many problems among the other staff because of her attitude. How can I write an honest but fair reference?

You should attempt to write only truthful statements in a reference and if you are asked outright questions about her ability to work in a team, you will have to say that this was probably not a strength she showed while working with you. It is only right to stress the things that she was good at – her ability to grasp new skills perhaps, her competence with computer in-putting, her facility with difficult patients – but you also have to hint at her weaknesses if you are to be fair to her new employer, and to her. After all you will not necessarily be doing her a service if you recommend her for a job for which she is quite obviously temperamentally unsuited. You can only comment on *your* experience of the individual, however, and you should point out in all fairness that it might only have been your team that she did not fit into and that in different circumstances she might fit in rather better.

When I had problems with a particular member of staff who had only been with us a few months, I telephoned one of her referees at her previous employment and asked if they had experienced similar problems when she worked for them. They had not mentioned any problems when I contacted them for a reference at the time of her appointment but conceded that they had indeed experienced similar problems but had not realized until now that she was to blame. With the benefit of hindsight, they now realized that when she left, so did the particular problem; they had given me a perfectly fair reference as they saw it at the time. When my turn came to give a reference for the same individual, I found it much harder to be fair without prejudicing her chances of future employment.

▲ Question 61: Writing reports

The last time I wrote anything longer than a personal letter, it was an essay at school. Can you give me some tips on writing reports?

There is a need in general practice, as in any other business, for concise reporting. GPs are busy people and have neither the time, nor indeed the inclination, to wade through wordy documents. In fact some practice managers summarize DoH edicts, health authority reports or other non-clinical papers for the doctors. You need to learn how to write succinctly, picking out only those matters of relevance using words sparingly and avoiding the temptation to add superfluous detail in an attempt to make the passage more interesting. Use simple words – a report is not the place to impress people with your wide vocabulary. Avoid jargon and abbreviations unless they are known to the reader and when using an abbreviation write it first in full with the abbreviated version in brackets. Subsequently you can use just the abbreviation.

Financial reports will obviously include figures. Make sure that any tables you use are self-explanatory and simple to understand – the whole point of a table or graph is to present facts clearly and reduce the number of words required. Diagrams can be another useful way of reducing the need for text.

Whatever you write, make sure that the following three components are always present:

1 clarity
2 brevity
3 accuracy.

Writing a report is not so very different from summarizing an important document and you still need to do the research, identify facts that need to be included and reject those matters that are not strictly relevant. If you start by deciding just what is the purpose of the report you are about to write, this should help you to concentrate on the facts that need to be included. Are you writing a feasibility study, project report or financial report for the previous 12 months? The purpose of some reports is merely to inform the reader of the circumstances and as such it should provide a summary of the facts, together with impartial arguments for and against a proposed course of action. Alternatively, a report might be intended to persuade in which case conclusions drawn from the facts will be required. You should end such a report by making recommendations.

Whatever the type of report it is helpful if a sequence of events is followed through logically. This could be a chronological, geographical or priority sequence. Each fact should be dealt with in order and if you adopt a logical structure to your documents, it will help draw the reader through to the conclusion.

The use of headings is essential. Main headings and sub-headings help to break up the text and allow skim readers to pick out the salient facts fast. For example, a feasibility report for ways of reducing the pressure on the current practice premises might take the form of:

- Introduction – status quo
- Aims and objectives – to find ways of reducing pressure on use of premises
- Main body of text – exploration of all the different possibilities including opening a branch, expanding the present building, moving to a new site, etc
- Conclusions – how cost-effective the different options are
- Recommendations – which option seems the most advantageous
- Summary.

Be prepared to draft and re-draft important documents. Leaving the first draft overnight and coming to it fresh the following day can lead to many useful amendments – superfluous words can be omitted, and important facts may come to mind that had been previously overlooked.

▲ Question 62: Annual report

In past years one of the GPs has compiled the annual report and the secretary has typed it. This year I have been asked to prepare the whole thing. Help!

Your health authority will probably require a report containing specified information about the practice for each financial year (April–March) which must be with them by the end of June. The required information will probably include:

A details of outside clinical commitments, including any hospital posts held by the GPs, together with the annual hourly commitment devoted to each activity

B arrangements the practice makes for repeat prescriptions to patients

C details of referrals of patients as inpatients or outpatients by specialty and the name of the hospital concerned

D the total number of self-referrals of which the doctor is aware (again by clinical specialty)

E information relating to the numbers of patients on the doctor's list who fulfil the following criteria:
   – they are diabetic
   – they are asthmatic
   – they have received advice on healthy living (tobacco usage, alcohol consumption and a weight check)

F the number of complaints received and dealt with under the in-house practice complaints procedure.

The information in section A only needs to be given if the doctors have changed their commitment from previous years. Details of referrals (sections C and D) are only required if the health authority directly requests the information and cannot obtain it from elsewhere. Details in section E only need to be supplied if the practice is not already supplying the information in order to qualify for health promotion payments.

All you have to do now is ensure that all the relevant information is with the health authority by the deadline at the end of June each year.

▲ Question 63: Partnership agreement

The doctors in our practice do not have a partnership agreement. Should they?

It is essential that the partners have an agreement because without one they are controlled by a century-old statute, the Partnership Act 1890. Without a written agreement, they become a 'partnership at will', the main features of which are:

- one partner can elect to end the partnership without notice, unless the remaining partners choose to continue
- the partnership will end automatically on the death or retirement of any one partner
- all partners must have free access to the bank account and are entitled to participate in the management of the business
- none of the partners can be expelled from the partnership
- most partnership decisions can be made by a majority of the partners, with the exception of the selection of a new partner or change in the nature of the business, which must be agreed by *all* the existing partners
- partners may not compete with the partnership; any income derived from outside activities in the same general field should be paid to the partnership

- all the partners are regarded as 'agents' of the partnership and can make decisions and enter into commitments to which the partnership is then bound.

GP partnerships are increasingly coming under pressure as more and more changes are being forced on them and the opportunities for disagreement between individual partners increases. Although a written agreement does not mean that problems will not occur, at least it provides a foundation for working out disagreements.

A written agreement should ensure equity for the partners and give them a basic security. In the event of a partner retiring or resigning, a new one joining, or a major change regarding premises or ownership, the written agreement will offer guidelines as to what the partners can reasonably expect. Matters such as arrangements for sabbaticals, maternity leave, sick leave, profit sharing and banking can all be covered in the agreement and should prevent misunderstandings.

For further details on how to go about creating a partnership agreement, you might like to refer to Chapter 5 of *General Practitioners Handbook*.[1]

▲ Question 64: Practice Charter

Do we really have to produce a Practice Charter?

Practices are required by the DoH to display a Practice Charter in the surgery and to make copies available to any patient who requests a copy. The charter should list all the duties that the practice accepts regarding access to GPs: availability of appointments, maximum waiting times, arrangements for repeat prescriptions, night visits, how to inform the practice of a change of address, availability of a complaints procedure, attitude of staff and doctors towards patients and so on. Many practices have also taken the opportunity to emphasize that just as the practice has a duty of care to their patients and will treat them as individuals with courtesy and respect, patients also have an obligation to respect the doctors and staff. They can be reminded about the importance of keeping appointments punctually and cancelling them when they are not required.

Dr John Chisholm, the current chairman of the BMA General Medical Services Committee, advised GPs in 1993 to 'concentrate on quality, not quantity or timings in their charters and to set realistic targets for the service they wish to offer. Standards should not be publicised unless they can be achieved.' For instance, if the charter states that the practice will guarantee a non-urgent appointment within three days and an urgent appointment the same day with a GP (but not necessarily the patient's own doctor), it could also state that patients themselves have a duty to inform the practice if they are unable to keep an appointment so that it can be offered to someone else.[19]

Many feel that charters have merely served to increase the demands made by patients on the health service. Perhaps we can go some way to redressing the balance by stating the practice's side and insisting on reasonable behaviour from the patients.

The government has recently come to the same conclusion and is intent on revising the Patients' Charter to include details of patients' obligations as well as their rights. It is hoped that this will help the process of educating patients and persuade them to have more realistic expectations of just what the NHS can provide.

▲ Question 65: Patient satisfaction surveys

We would like to know whether our patients believe we are living up to the ideals of our Practice Charter. How can we set about doing a survey of our patients?

One of the least expensive ways of asking patients if they are happy with the services you offer at the practice, is to give them a questionnaire to fill in while they wait for their appointment. For such a survey, you are likely to be most interested in those patients who attend the surgery frequently, rather than those who never come. Catching them opportunistically would seem a useful way of discovering their views.

You should prepare the questionnaire with care, ensuring that you do not ask leading questions. If you use tick boxes, then the questions will elicit only a 'yes' or 'no' reply, but if you leave space for longer responses, then it gives you the chance to put some open questions. You could ask for suggestions for improvements to the waiting area or the treatment room service, rather than just seek to know whether the patients are happy with the current arrangements.

If you want to seek the opinions of patients who seldom attend the surgery, you will have to conduct a mailshot and either choose a random sample of patients (not as easy as it sounds) or send a questionnaire to all the patients on the list. Make sure that both sexes and all ages and socio-economic groups are represented if you want to select a sample group; this is not always possible to do with any degree of accuracy in what is likely to be a relatively small sample. Once again you must prepare the questionnaire very carefully to avoid any bias in the questions and it is helpful to identify in advance exactly what information you are seeking.

Collation of the results can be very time-consuming but it is a task that you can delegate to an outside agency or one of the other staff in the practice. Once you have established the results, post details of what you have ascertained on a noticeboard in the practice and state what actions the practice is planning to take as a result of all this research. Patients will be more willing to fill in such questionnaires in future if they can see that you are acting on the results.

▲ Question 66: Suggestion box

No one ever puts suggestions in our box at reception. Can you give me some ideas of how to increase interest among patients in having a say about the services we offer at the practice?

As patients often feel embarrassed at putting notes in the box in view of the receptionists, fearing that people will think they are making a complaint, it might be better to move the box away from the main desk and out of sight of the staff. By placing the box in a less conspicuous place, you might find the occasional sweet wrapper but you are also more likely to receive some useful suggestions.

You could try promoting to the patients the fact that the practice would welcome suggestions as to how they feel that services could be improved. This can be done by placing posters around the practice and putting a paragraph in the practice newsletter, if you have one, or the practice brochure which should be available at reception. You could ask the GPs and nurses at the end of a consultation to suggest to patients that they might like to put any comments in writing (anonymously if they so wish) when they have something they particularly want to say. The incentive for the patient is to know that something is likely to be done about their suggestion if it is in writing, rather than just a verbal comment made to one of the staff.

▲ Question 67: Complaints procedure

We have a complaints procedure within the practice but I am not sure that it complies with statutory requirements. Exactly what should we be doing?

It is a terms of service requirement that every practice has a complaints procedure to which patients can be directed if they have a complaint. First of all, you need to inform patients that such a procedure is in operation in the practice by advertising this on a poster in the waiting area, in the practice brochure and on leaflets prominently displayed at reception.

The protocol should include details of the named person in the practice to whom patients should make their complaint in the first instance – this is likely to be the practice manager, although it does not have to be. All complaints must be made in writing by a patient or on behalf of a patient. A written record should be kept of the nature of the complaint, any letter or verbal contact should be acknowledged in writing within a period of three working days and the complaint must be investigated fully. The complaints officer will wish to interview the complainant and then hear the other side of the story by talking to the doctor or member of staff who is the subject of the complaint.

If the matter is relatively trivial it may be sufficient to inform the patient of your findings, express sympathy for their distress and if appropriate offer an apology. Many complainants just want some acknowledgement that they are justified in feeling aggrieved and a simple apology will usually suffice. For more serious matters, the patient may insist that you refer the matter to the health authority which could lead to a detailed investigation and a tribunal. However, this should be a last resort since the business is protracted and stressful both for the patient and for the doctor against whom the complaint is being made.

In-house complaints procedures have reduced the number of formal complaints going to tribunal in recent years and so practices should embrace their system as a way of diffusing potentially damaging situations quickly and effectively. For further details you should contact your health authority to find out their exact requirements for the current year.

▲ Question 68: Practice leaflets

I understand we have to produce a practice leaflet for distribution to our patients. How can we do this cost-effectively?

In the early 1990s the Government made it a requirement that GPs produce a practice leaflet to provide patients with the information:

- details, both professional and personal, of the doctors including:
  - full name
  - sex
  - qualifications registered by the GMC
  - date and place of first registration as a medical practitioner
  - whether they work part-time, full-time, job-sharing, single-handed or in a group practice
  - the times during which the GPs are personally available for consultation by patients at the surgery
  - whether there is an appointments system and, if so, the method of obtaining urgent and non-urgent appointments
  - how the patient should obtain a home visit
  - the doctors' arrangements for providing cover when he is not available
  - how to obtain repeat prescriptions (and dispensed medication for dispensing practices)
  - frequency, duration and purpose of any clinics
  - the numbers of employed staff and a description of their roles in the practice
  - details of whether the GPs provide such services as maternity, contraceptive, child health surveillance or minor surgery
  - the geographical boundary of the practice illustrated with a small sketch map
  - whether the premises are accessible to patients in wheelchairs
  - details of whether the practice is a GP training practice and/or undertakes the teaching of undergraduate medical students.

Together with all this statutory information, many practices choose to include a section on how to treat common ailments such as coughs and colds, flu and gastric upsets.

There are several ways of producing a suitable practice leaflet and various companies, such as Neighbourhood Direct, who produce brochures for GP surgeries free of charge. A member of their staff visits the practice for a week or two to telephone around local businesses to drum up sufficient advertising to cover the cost of producing several thousand copies of the brochure. Do be aware that local businesses are often reluctant to take out expensive advertising that is perceived to be of little value to them. It is therefore useful to suggest the names of local businesses to the salesman so that he can target specific companies that might benefit from having their name put before the likely readers, namely mothers of young children and elderly people. You also have to ensure that you retain the right of veto and can refuse advertisements you consider inappropriate for publication in a surgery leaflet.

Alternatively, you can keep costs down by producing the leaflet yourself using desktop publishing. Perhaps a few local companies might agree to buy advertising space. Also, national concerns like PPA, BUPA and Nuffield Hospitals sometimes take out such advertisements.

Don't forget that you are required to state the sex of all the GPs. Some practices have fallen foul of this regulation by assuming that a masculine or feminine first name would be sufficient notification of the doctor's gender. Not so. M or F should always appear beside the name to denote the sex.

▲ Question 69: The practice newsletter/ bulletin

We want to find a way of keeping our patients informed of changes in services at the practice. How can we go about this on a regular basis?

A practice newsletter or bulletin is one way you can do this. Reminders about 'flu injections, the imminent hay fever season and news of practice developments (building works, a new partner, changes in staff) can all be included in it. Patients might also like to be kept informed of any doctor or member of staff who has married recently or had a baby. It is relatively easy to produce such a newsletter in-house, using desktop publishing or a word-processor. It need only be one or two sides of A4, perhaps arranged in two columns and depending on the amount of news you find to report, it can be produced quarterly, bi-monthly or even monthly.

It is more eye-catching if the newsletter is printed on coloured paper, perhaps a different colour for each edition so that patients can tell at a glance whether they have seen the particular issue. You can then photocopy the number of copies required, display the newsletter in reception and place a poster in the waiting-room informing patients of its existence, you will probably reach the majority of patients who attend the surgery.

But what of those who seldom come? If the news you have is sufficiently important, you might consider mailing all patients a copy. Addresses can be obtained by mail-merging the patient database – you cannot, of course, allow for those patients who might already have obtained a copy from reception. An alternative to posting copies which can be time-consuming and expensive, is to hire people to deliver copies for you throughout the more densely populated areas of the practice. Those living in the outlying districts can receive postal copies.

▲ Question 70: Item of service Links

We have successfully implemented registration links and are now facing items of service Links. Have you any advice on how we can avoid some of the problems that other practices have experienced in installing this?

If you have had registration Links for some time, you will by now have realized what a boon it can be when it works well. At its best it is a fast and efficient system that requires little active management but people's experience of item of service Links has been rather different, especially in the initial phases of introduction. Some practices have even been tempted to revert to paper claims, such is their disillusionment.

It is important that the practice understands the cycle of claims and health authority closure dates which differ slightly from district to district. For example, child health surveillance (CHS) and contraceptive claims are dealt with as registration items and are processed to a different timescale to all other item of service claims. One way of ensuring that all relevant CHS claims are made is to check your under-fives list and make sure that you have made a claim for any newly-registered children on the list in this age group.

It is helpful if you monitor regularly various items such as immunizations given in the practice and identify any that have not been claimed in the quarter. Don't forget that there is no flexibility over timing with the new system – you cannot send in overdue claims as you could with the manual system. It should be possible on most systems to set up stored searches which can be made on all the different types of claim at regular intervals and this should ensure you do not overlook any that are outstanding. Maternity claims are potentially so valuable that some practices prefer to keep a duplicate manual system so that they can cross-reference and ensure that none of the relevant data is missed off the claim.

It is important to send claims in on a regular basis, rather than save them up for just before the cut-off date. Allow not only for problems with your own software but also for the health authority closing down their system for maintenance at a crucial moment.

▲ Question 71: GP/provider Links

I understand that most practices will soon have pathology links and that it will be expanded to include pathology and radiology requests as well as just the results. Can you tell me how it will work?

The GP/provider Links started with electronic transmission of pathology and radiology results and discharge letters. It is now being expanded to include requests for tests, outpatient attendance reports and notifications of admissions to hospital, as well as notification of any deaths.

A pilot was run in Bristol in 1996 where a practice received all pathology and radiology results electronically and these were downloaded on to the computer system direct from the hospital. The practice then programmed its software to ensure that all normal results were filed automatically in the patient's notes, leaving only the abnormal ones to be viewed by the GP. The doctor could then take the relevant action and write a prescription or instruct staff to book an appointment for the patient to see either the doctor or a nurse.

Links between providers and purchasers are the way forward and once the system is well established, the saving of reception time in pulling notes and filing results will be considerable.

References

1 Ellis N (ed.) (1997) *General Practitioners Handbook.* Radcliffe Medical Press, Oxford.
2 Longridge L (1997) The corner chemist. *Practice Manager.* 7: 11–12.
3 Belbin RM (1981) *Management Teams.* Heinemann, Oxford.
4 Irvine S and Haman H (1997) *Making Sense of Personnel Management* (2nd ed.). Radcliffe Medical Press, Oxford.
5 Tyson S and York A (1993) *Personnel Management* (2nd ed.). Butterworth-Heinemann, Oxford.
6 Herzberg F (1968) One more time: how do you motivate employees? *Harvard Business Review.* **46**.
7 Jenks JM and Kelly JM (1985) *Don't Do. Delegate!* (2nd ed.). Kogan Page, London.
8 Stewart R (1986) *The Reality of Management.* Pan Books, London.
9 Irvine D and Irvine S (1996) *The Practice of Quality.* Radcliffe Medical Press, Oxford.
10 Brooks J and Borgardts I (1994) *Total Quality in General Practice.* Radcliffe Medical Press, Oxford.

11 Irvine D and Irvine S (1997) *Making Sense of Audit* (2nd ed.). Radcliffe Medical Press, Oxford.

12 Chambers C, Coopey J and McLean A (1990) *Develop your Management Potential*. Kogan Page, London.

13 Longridge L (1997) *General Practice Manager Briefing*. Issue **21**. Croner, Kingston-upon-Thames.

14 Adams J, Hayes J and Hopson B (1976) *Transition: understanding and managing personal change*. Blackwells, Oxford.

15 Huntington J (1995) *Managing the Practice: whose business?* Radcliffe Medical Press, Oxford.

16 Longridge L (1997) *General Practice Manager Special Report: running effective practice meetings*. Issue **13**. Croner, Kingston-upon-Thames.

17 Montgomery R (1968) *The Truth About Success and Motivation*. Thorsons Publishing Group, Wellingborough.

18 Buzan T (1987) *Use Your Head*. BBC Books, London.

19 Chisholm J (1993) Rights imply responsibilities. *Medical Monitor*. 7: 25.

Further reading

Adair J (1985) *Effective Decision-making*. Pan Books, London.

Adair J (1983) *Effective Leadership*. Pan Books, London.

Baker R and Presley P (1990) *The Practice Audit Plan: a handbook of medical audit*. RCGP Severn Faculty, Bristol.

Handy C (1985) *Understanding Organizations*. (2nd ed.). Penguin, Harmondsworth.

Handy C (1990) *Inside Organizations*. BBC Books, London.

Hudson M (1995) *Managing Without Profit*. Penguin Books, London.

Irvine D (1990) *Managing for Quality in General Practice*. King's Fund, London.

Macdonald J (1986) *Climbing the Ladder: how to be a woman manager*. Methuen, London.

Ovreteit J (1992) *Health Service Quality*. Blackwells, Oxford.

RCGP (1985) *Quality in General Practice. Policy Statement 2*. RCGP, London.

Stemp P (1988) *Are You Managing?* The Industrial Society, London.

Useful addresses

Association of Managers in General Practice (AMGP)
Suite 308
The Foundry
156 Blackfriars Road
London SE1 8EN
Tel: 0171 721 7080

Association of Medical Secretaries, Practice Administrators and Receptionists (AMSPAR)
Tavistock House North
Tavistock Square
London WC1H 9JR
Tel: 0171 387 6005

British Medical Association
BMA House
Tavistock Square
London WC1H 9JP
Tel: 0171 387 4499

Croner Publications Ltd
Croner House
London Road
Kingston-upon-Thames
Surrey KT2 6SR
Tel: 0181 547 3333
Fax: 0181 547 2637

McLean McNicoll Software
Erskine View Clinic
Old Kilpatric
Glasgow G60 5SJ
Ansaphone/Fax: 0141 952 9707

Medical Defence Union
3 Devonshire Place
London W1N 2EA
Tel: 0171 486 6181

Medical Protection Society
Granary Wharf House
Leeds LS11 5PY
Tel: 0113 243 6436

Neighbourhood Direct Ltd
Keenans Mill
Lord Street
St Annes-on-Sea
Lancashire F78 2DF
Tel: 01253 722142

Radcliffe Medical Press Ltd (for PRP course)
18 Marcham Road
Abingdon
Oxon OX14 1AA
Tel: 01235 528820

Royal College of General Practitioners (RCGP)
14 Princes Gate
Hyde Park
London SW7 1PU
Tel: 0171 581 3232
Fax: 0171 225 3046

Royal College of Nursing (RCN)
20 Cavendish Square
London W1M 9AE
Tel: 0171 409 3333

Sterling Events (conference organizers)
62 Hope Street
Liverpool L1 9BZ
Tel: 0151 709 7979
Fax: 0151 709 0384

Index

For Product Safety Concerns and Information please contact our EU
representative GPSR@taylorandfrancis.com
Taylor & Francis Verlag GmbH, Kaufingerstraße 24, 80331 München, Germany

www.ingramcontent.com/pod-product-compliance
Ingram Content Group UK Ltd.
Pitfield, Milton Keynes, MK11 3LW, UK
UKHW020946180425
457613UK00019B/543